To Paul —
my dear friend
& environmental
buddy

Scoop
11-24-15

INSIDE THE
ARKANSAS
LEGISLATURE

INSIDE THE ARKANSAS LEGISLATURE

Bill "Scoop" Lancaster

To order additional copies of this book, contact:
Xlibris
1-888-795-4274
www.Xlibris.com
Orders@Xlibris.com
712389

Mr. Witt, thanks for introducing me to politics, and for my first limo ride.

INTRODUCTION

J ohn Wayne is my number 1 hero, Andy Griffith a close second. I mention *the Duke* here only because I remembered a quote from his daughter, Aissa, when I started to put this book together. Upon her father's death, she talked about how movie moguls mistreated her dad. "There's some real SOBs in this business," she said of Hollywood.

I'd put some former members of the Arkansas legislature in that same dreadful category—rapacious SOBs sprinkled liberally among a host of gifted and talented good-government advocates. And I mention the Mayberry sheriff because the late senator Bill Gwatney once referred to me as the Andy Griffith of the Arkansas Senate in paying me what I considered the ultimate compliment. At the time, *Gwatzilla* (his nickname) was telling colleagues how I quietly consoled those around me while putting others in the spotlight, just as Andy did with Barney and the unmanageable gang on the old TV show. I never had a little brother, and I always thought of Bill Gwatney that way, as did all of us in the Mike Beebe "Worm Club." My friend Don Tilton, who became a high-dollar lobbyist, always introduced me as "the straw that stirs the drink," and I got a kick out of that too.

This book is my recollection of twenty-six years at the Arkansas State Capitol. My jobs were information director/assistant coordinator of the Arkansas House of Representatives and chief of staff of the Arkansas Senate. I started putting these thoughts down years ago, saving notes and photos, talking with various individuals, and I hadn't thought anymore about pursuing the idea of a book until Governor Beebe encouraged me to go for it. He said there weren't many of us still alive with "institutional knowledge" of how the Arkansas General Assembly existed prior to term limits, and he suggested, there might be a worthwhile reason to jot down some reflections of those long-ago days. I always did what Mike urged me to do because, well, he gave sound advice, and quite honestly, if it hadn't been for him and a little meeting in 1985 at the Flaming Arrow Supper Club in Little Rock, I never would have been an integral part of the Arkansas Senate in the first place.

I worked with some great folks inside the Arkansas legislature, but certainly some were not so great and merited watching. As one dying senator whispered to me on his deathbed as he pulled me close, "Listen to me—you be careful, you hear me. Some of those people out there will cut your throat and watch you bleed to death."

The man who said that was Tom Watson, a nice, quiet senator from East Arkansas who passed away far too soon in his career. I sat with him at the hospital, and as you can see, I never forgot his terrifying warning. Imagine saying that to someone, knowing you would never see them again. Better still, imagine my angst as I listened, but I knew these dying words were to be taken seriously, and they were.

My work was a fun, roller-coaster adventure with lots of ups and downs. I almost got fired twice: once for defending William Parks, a young black employee, against what I saw as a deplorable racist policy, and another time, much later down my career path, after I was accused of saying disparaging things about some term-limited, thin-skinned senators in a newspaper column. One lawmaker mentioned in the column was Jodie Mahony of El Dorado, one of the very best legislators ever, in my opinion. More about this controversy later in the book, and I'll name my all-time favorite legislators, and as a bit of a preview, I'll say now that Mahony was one of those.

Over my career, I dealt with bureaucrats, politicians, lobbyists, reporters, and the public. I traveled to exotic places and historical sites, and I made friends with men and women of every political persuasion. I ate triple-buttered popcorn with the Clintons, chicken-fried steaks with Bob Dole, Sims barbecue with Jesse Jackson, and foot-long hot dogs with Arnold Schwarzenegger, and I golfed with governors, college presidents, Razorback coaches, and PGA pros while coordinating schedules and running the show for my Senate bosses—some of whom became lifelong friends. Our golfing adventures became well-known at the capitol and in print, and Senator Nick Wilson, an archenemy of Beebe, sarcastically dubbed us the Young Golfers. I even hosted a golf event of my own, and dozens of lawmakers, including US Senator David Pryor and big-name college coaches, rolled into my hometown and partied down at my house in Sheridan.

I was privileged to take a leadership role in the Southern Legislative Conference, which allowed me to serve as moderator of national debates featuring leading politicians and reporters. I watched tinhorn senators like Mike Ross grow into national leaders while others more capable and much more courageous than Ross fell from grace and power and shuffled off to prison. Along the way, I fought my way back from a life-threatening injury; I helped save a young senator's life by giving him mouth-to-mouth, and I carried another veteran legislator in my arms to the hospital to die.

I learned over a quarter of a century that there is a cyclical nature to politics, that new ideas and new problems rarely surface, and that senators and representatives seldom plow new ground, dealing with the same recurring issues year in and year out—education, prisons, highways, and health. This explains why politicians and, yes, the legal system just can't leave things alone. Issues like abortion and voting rights continually show back up in lawmaking bodies and court jurisdictions. Fact is, most Arkansans don't give a damn about politics except when they need something for themselves and/or they're too cheap to hire a lawyer.

Fat-cat special interests can control the political agenda in Arkansas, and big money talks. I found that out firsthand. And regrettably, I saw that proselytizing radical fundamentalists do indeed get elected to the House and Senate every once in a while, though they usually self-destruct once they get there.

I met a lot of nice governors along the way. David Pryor, who officially left the governor's office shortly before I arrived, was the most popular and told the best stories. His prizewinner is about two former legislators—senators Jack Gibson of Boydell (one of my favorites) and Dooley Womack of Camden. These two senators were in Las Vegas at a convention when a reporter asked Gibson what he thought of euthanasia. A quick wit, Jack responded, "Hell, she's a little old, but she looks pretty damned good for a stripper."

I thought Governor Jim Guy Tucker, a Harvard graduate, was hardworking. He'd work late at night and take two briefcases home with him. I guess it was all government work—hope it didn't deal with those complicated matters that finally got him in trouble with the law.

Bill Clinton was erratic in his first term but got better after the jovial Frank White taught him a lesson in humility. Frank was charitable and put together a talented staff, and Mike Huckabee was a ton of fun at informal gatherings at Cecil Alexander's house when he joined Mike Beebe in some serious guitar pickin'. And Huckabee kept an honest-to-goodness Arkansas historian, Rex Nelson, on his staff to help straighten out occasional messes.

The Senate staff I put together helped senators deal with legislative issues and personal problems. I went to work as the Senate's first chief of staff in 1985, thanks to then senator Mike Beebe, and I stayed there until 2004, when I quietly walked out of my fancy office one sunny afternoon and returned home to Sheridan to take a new job at the Witt Stephens Grant County Museum. I never returned to the capitol building after that, and I honestly never missed any of it—the dreadfully long legislative sessions, the dishonesty, the knives in the back. And from what I heard from friends and associates, including Mike Beebe and Morril Harriman, I wouldn't have enjoyed being at the capitol during the extended term-limited era anyway. Much of the trust factor, which was always strained but still present at times, disappeared after term limits made veteran legislators extinct. At least, this is what legislators and lobbyists told me later on.

In 1959, I was thirteen years old when I confided in a childhood friend that I wanted to grow up one day and become a person whom people went to for advice. I don't know why I said that at such an early age, but I did, and looking back now on my time inside the Arkansas legislature and dealing with others in politics, I see clearly that my boyhood wish did, indeed, come true as I rose through the ranks and moved to one of the top positions in Arkansas state government. Leaders sought my advice on problems that confronted them, and they listened to me in the private moments too, sometimes over a late-afternoon cocktail, in private backroom dinners at Doe's, riding in a golf cart at the remarkable Greenbrier resort, or just relaxing with a rod and reel in the middle of Wayne Hampton's beautiful reservoir. I take comfort now in old age, believing that they listened to me because of a trust factor that you don't always see in bureaucrats. I always spoke my mind, and what I spoke wasn't always what my bosses wanted to hear. I still take pride in that.

Ray Thornton is a close friend, and I worked for him once in my career. He's known best for his years in Congress, but he also served on the state supreme court and as president of our two leading public universities. He told me he liked our private conversations, which he called Sheridan talk, because he could always count on me to tell him the truth.

"I used to get so mad at you," he told me once. "But then I would be driving home, and I would realize that you were one of the few people who would tell me what I needed to hear instead of what I wanted to hear."

That meant a lot to me because I hold Ray Thornton, an old Sheridan friend, in high esteem. He was one of the most honest people I knew in politics, and our state benefitted greatly from his service.

Charlie Cole Chaffin, a fine state senator from Benton, was one of the very best too, and *she*—yes, Charlie is female—she said there weren't enough guts among Arkansas lawmakers to feed a quail a chitlin supper. I believe that too, and that certainly was true when it came to the people who worked for the legislators.

Tim Massanelli, who helped train me in my years at the House, had a big ego, but he also had the courage to speak up and speak out when he dealt with his legislative bosses, and I learned from watching him.

And I had my newspaper career, which prepared me well for my work in politics because when you are a reporter for a big newspaper—and the *Arkansas Gazette* was very big before it turned to mush—well, you learn that you better stand up for what you believe in, or you'll be stampeded.

Refusing to budge on principle got me a few hours in a jail cell once in my newspaper career. It happened in DeWitt during my coverage of a murder trial. The prosecutor was a friend, and he invited me into the judge's chambers to hear pretrial motions. In those days, the *Gazette* was revered, and its reporters were well-known. The presiding judge didn't take too kindly to me being in there, even though the prosecutor tried to explain that he had issued the invitation. The judge said the room's window air conditioner wasn't working properly and that I would have to leave. I responded that he didn't have to come up with a lame excuse if he wanted me out, and then one thing led to another, and I ended up behind bars for a few hours until the *Gazette* lawyer made a phone call, and the local sheriff cut me loose.

So that being said, back to politics.

I remember my first sit-down meeting with new senator Jim Hill of Nashville. He asked me to join him in a drive-over to a duck club where we were invited to hunt. Jim had just been sworn in at the Senate, and he said the time together would give us a chance to talk. On the way, he asked why he had been denied an apartment at the Capitol Hill building. This was a building adjacent the Capitol, and he had asked to be considered if apartment space became available. At the time, the senators with seniority or who were closely associated with Senator Nick Wilson were most likely to be chosen by the secretary of state to get an apartment.

"I want to be honest with you," I explained to the new senator. "I'm probably the reason you didn't get picked." The reason, I went on, was that senators Steve Bell and Joe Yates were moving into a two-bedroom apartment, and I helped them get the larger space because I wanted to room part-time with them. This decision set into motion other renovation plans that eventually meant Hill wouldn't be chosen. So I told him, I might be the very person to actually blame if he wanted to blame anyone for his failure to get a room.

"You didn't have to tell me that," he said in a surprised tone.

"Senator Hill, I won't ever lie to you," I assured him because that was my personal code in doing my job at the Senate.

I had thirty-five bosses, some of whom hated their own colleagues, and I knew, going in in 1985, that I would always have to stand my ground, speak my mind, and answer truthfully. And I always did that. As for others who worked there, I'd refer you back to Charlie Cole Chaffin's quote. Few staffers took risks and spoke their mind, most were overly timid, and they tried their best to stay out of sight in order not to rock a boat. Job security was their main goal, and I'd have to say most of them were awfully good at it.

I met some great people who taught me a lot. I learned about fine wines, political compromise, the beauty of art, the wonders of travel, the craftiness of politics, and the heartache associated with personal and professional failure. I made a ton of mistakes in my personal and professional life, but I earned enough money to build a nice home and get my kids a good education, and I always, always tried to professionally represent the Arkansas Senate.

I put up with a lazy, insipid columnist who had trouble with his facts and another who admitted he didn't always check his facts when he wrote his own inaccurate articles. Unbelievably, one of them wrote that I was away on a Sunday outing at a duck club when I was at home in Sheridan and serving communion at my church. The minister asked me how a reporter could write such horrible things, and I told him not to fret, that people in my line of work were used to such paparazzi antics and acutely aware of the deteriorating reputation of the press. I told the minister to remember the Good Book's lessons on forgiveness and let the issue pass, which he did. But I also dealt with professional journalists who did get it right—Bill Simmons and Carol Griffee to name two who, I thought, were a credit to their craft.

The two biggest changes in the Arkansas political landscape that I witnessed were Jay Bradford's stunning defeat of Knox Nelson in 1991 and the passage of the term limits amendment in 1992. Senator Bradford's defeat of the Senate's kingpin changed the face of Arkansas politics. Weeks later, Senator Max Howell, the other kingpin and Nelson's right-hand man, announced his retirement, knowing that he would be the next toothless tiger to fall. Then term limits changed what was left, literally wiping out more than a thousand years of experience overnight in the two chambers. "Experienced legislator" would no longer be a term in Arkansas's political lexicon. The paradigm had shifted, and regrettably to some, there was no turning back. Forever, the Natural State would have no "naturals" in the well of the chamber, extolling the virtues of a bill, articulating as Lloyd George, Buddy Turner, and Wayne Dowd had done so artfully over the years. It appeared that the House and Senate would be lacking the gravitas of the past, saddled instead with computer geeks, e-mailers, and term-limited, abortion-crazed advocates who were pristine and politically correct, holed up in the Heights, sipping a latte instead of ordering up another round of big-boy drinks at the Flaming Arrow. Advocates of the old style would be asking: Where had all the real men like John Wayne and Andy Griffith gone? Like me, they boarded the slow train out of Little Rock and retired to the quiet life.

CHAPTER 1

State Representative Napoleon Bonaparte Murphy Jr. stumbled his way to center stage, and three thousand legislators and guests craned for a better view. Zorro-like, he unfurled his famous fiddle and reached nervously for the microphone.

That was when reality hit like a Sonny Liston uppercut. I would have to be the one to take action. No one else had the balls to extract the familiar intruder, yank him off the stage, and try to salvage the musical finale that had been meticulously choreographed to move Little Rock into the national limelight.

Understand, it was not unusual for N. B. "Nap" Murphy of LA (Lower Arkansas) to show up at parties after several tantalizing "refreshments" and pull out his fabled fiddle. In fact, it was unusual when he did not magically appear. A few years after the debacle that was unfolding this balmy night in 1987 at Little Rock's amphitheater, he would be promptly *escorted* by the Secret Service from Bill Clinton's White House lawn for pissin' on the presidential shrubbery.

A lot of people liked ol' Nap, and he could be extremely charming, but the aging legislator's late-night antics had worn thin over the years. Sadly, he had become a comédie larmoyante for the Arkansas General Assembly, and by the time his career petered out in the late 1980s, he was public relations enemy number 1 for me and the legislature, regrettably placed in the same pathetic class as some others with whom I had to deal.

For every decent and honorable member of the 135-member assembly, there always seemed to be a handful of buffoons and slimeballs who deep-sixed the legislature's would-be progressive image. Even before the Nick Wilson crime wave rolled across the Senate in 1999, there were sufficient numbers of self-inflicted wounds that periodically damaged the institution's public image. The press loved to write about the occasional faux pas and blunder, and who could blame them? Arkansas legislators were masters at self-destruction.

Nap, for instance. The pride of Hamburg was a photogenic, brilliant businessman who became a fixture at the legislature from 1963 until 1995. But as the legislature changed and attempted to get serious about Bumpers-Pryor-Clinton era challenges to improve government, fewer and fewer legislative colleagues remained tolerant of Nap and his fiddling escapades.

As Clinton was moving into his second term as governor in 1983, having dethroned the gregarious Frank White, the legislature showed more and more encouraging signs of becoming progressive, willing to accept new ideas while shucking some of its questionable past. The born-again young governor had asked the public's forgiveness for a Cubans-and-car-tag-marred first run, and he was returning to the capitol with newfound gusto.

The legislature's image was changing too. Better staff was being hired as patronage slowly gave way to qualifications. Progressive leaders like Mike Beebe and John Paul Capps were making their voices heard above legislators labeled by the press as perennial bullies. Little Rock's newspaper war was helping shape the new image too, as capitol beat reporters scripted more and more "personality" pieces. It was a sign of the times in society and in journalism—fluff over substance. Editors at the beleaguered *Arkansas Gazette* and ambitious *Arkansas Democrat* wanted more imagery, charts, and graphs—more on who was at the helm in state government. I was glad to help them from my new post as the Arkansas House information director. I had spent my career in journalism, and now I was on the other side of the fence, trying to handle public relations for political bosses while helping the hardworking reporters who wrote about these men and women.

Serious-minded legislators like John Miller and Mike Wilson wanted better tax programs and pay for teachers, and they talked about such things late at night with staff and administrators. Rock-solid legislators named Don Corbin and Jodie Mahony on the

Democratic side and Carolyn Pollan and Preston Bynum on the Republican side were coming into their own as aging dinosaurs with limited ability and incendiary tempers were shuffling toward the exits, old ideas and tired philosophies in tow.

Nap Murphy's embarrassing adventures, Representative Frank Willems's occasional clowning on the House floor, or Senator Bill Moore attempting to bilk taxpayers for illegal air travel reimbursements—well, there was no time for such high jinks in the minds of many new leaders.

I had worked almost seven years at the House of Representatives when the Senate finally convinced me in 1985 to go to work for them as their first chief of staff. I had been in my new job two years when the incident with ol' Nap occurred on the huge stage at the back of Little Rock's Excelsior Hotel.

It was a beautiful August night, and the curtain was coming down on the Forty-First Annual Southern Legislative Conference. The SLC is an organization of Southern states, and each year, the group convenes in a Southern city to discuss legislative issues and put on the feed bag. This year, it had been Arkansas's turn to host, and this was a big deal for the state and the city of Little Rock. Thousands of guests streamed into the capital city. Hotels were crammed; restaurants were bursting with high-dollar customers; and on top of all that, every presidential hopeful, from the diminutive Michael Dukakis to the flamboyant Jesse Jackson, had arrived to appear on national telecasts and charm convention delegates and the national press at a time when the Southern Regional Primary was becoming a huge factor in the presidential nomination process. Bottom line: things were hopping.

Laying the groundwork for the convention had been a massive undertaking. Key legislative staff had worked long hours. The venerable Tim Massanelli of the House staff and veteran budgeteer Bill Goodman of the legislative council had spent time with me at Fort Worth the previous summer, tracking how Texas officials had prepared to host the meeting in their state. After our long stay in the Lone Star State, we worked tirelessly to make sure transportation, accommodations, food, and entertainment were the absolute best for the meeting in Little Rock.

The big event that closes each SLC meeting is called the State
Dinner. This is usually a stuffy, black-tie affair that features a
stuffy, black-tied speaker. Arkansas organizers decided to do things
differently, and we hired Jason D. Williams, a spectacular rock-and-
roll singer, to cap an evening on the river that featured a family picnic
complete with Tyson chicken, Riceland rice, and Hope watermelons.
The melons, some weighing over fifty pounds, were delivered in
refrigerated eighteen-wheelers.

It had been a gigantic effort, but thanks to legislators like the
amiable Capps, we were able to arrange a social and cultural calendar
that presented a modern, progressive, forward-looking Arkansas to all
special visitors. In order to pull this off, however, John Paul and I had
to meet secretly with a paid consultant to make sure the entertainment
met our lofty standards. It wasn't that we thought we were any better
than others in the planning group, but John Paul and I shared a love
for our state that made us want a better image, and we knew that
this convention, with all the would-be presidents in town along with
national C-SPAN telecasts, could become a national showcase.

I told John Paul that I wanted the Arkansas Symphony and jazz
combos scattered around the picnic venue, and he heartily agreed. He
said he wanted a "sophisticated" approach to the entertainment, and I
knew exactly what he meant.

In one meeting, he and I held firm against a few hayseed legislators
and one veteran staffer who lobbied for Arkansas folksinger Jimmy
Driftwood and what I described as "clogger" entertainment. I insisted
on the symphony and other more upscale entertainment, even
though I knew I had pissed off some who saw my attitude as "typical
arrogance of the Senate." House members and some staff always
whispered that the senators were snobbish and that the entertainment
issue was typical of the way the Senate pushed the House around.
But they were wrong to believe that. My goal was to make the city
and state look good and to do my damnedest to keep people like
Jimmy Driftwood and the toothless Grandpa Jones squirreled away in
Branson or wherever.

The whole week had been splendid. All the presidential candidates
had visited, and I had watched over each of them at a private suite at
the beautiful Capital Hotel. C-SPAN broadcast many of the events

nationally, and many in the national press corps had offered up rave reviews about the city.

The picnic finale had debuted on a positive note too, as an unexpected cool front dropped the late-summer temps to humidity-free digits, and guests swarmed to the riverbank to eat and listen to symphonic music topped off with kick-ass tunes from Jason D. Williams.

A Smackover-area native, Williams was at the top of his performing game. He was noted for frequent visits to Arkansas, and he had begun to appear on prominent TV shows, including *Saturday Night Live*. This night in Little Rock, he was quick to bond with the huge crowd that had settled in at dusk. One song into the performance, and the crowd could see how he had earned his reputation as a rambunctious piano-playin' Jerry Lee Lewis clone. He was jumping all over the place, banging the piano, standing on the keyboard, and turning cartwheels in his chair. He was *the* man, bustin' his chops as the crowd roared its approval. Big, fat legislators were high-fiving staff; Alabama House members were hand jivin' and shakin' a tail feather—it was all coming together in glorious fashion. All of us who had worked for two years were delighted, not because we had pulled it off, but because people were loving Little Rock, something that made our low-self-esteemed Arkansas asses prouder than punch.

But then, out of nowhere, lightning flashes. Jason D pauses for a drink of water, and out of the clear blue walks the Arkansas legislature's ultimate nightmare. Colonel Sanders—white-suited, head-to-toe-fiddled-up, and alcohol-primed to "Orange Blossom Special" the hell out of delegates from Missouri to Panama Beach, none other than NAP MURPHY!

In my mind, I could hear 134 Arkansas legislators thinking *Oh, Lord!* Even the saintly John Miller was *almost probably* thinking about cussing. How in the world could this be happening? Forget Little Rock Central and its permanent stain on our reputation. Now, dozens of visiting journalists could resharpen their claws on the Natural State because of this cornpone Arkie in the zoot suit and patent leather shoes. I could see my new friend from the *Boston Globe* up on the hill, laughing, and I could picture his paper's next headline: **Lum and Abner Alive and Well on the ArKANSAS River.**

At first, the uneasy hush. No one, not a single soul, uttered a word. Arkansas legislators and staff sat in disbelief, bug-eyed, silent. Singer Jason D, ever cool, Elvis-like, stared at the elderly intruder, turning to the audience and gesturing with his arms to indicate he was not aware of what was going on. But the singer's expression changed suddenly, concerned perhaps about what Nap was removing from the weathered instrument case. Entertainers never know about threatening fans, and I became concerned that Williams might bolt, take matters into his own hands, and attack the elderly Murphy, who now was mumbling and twisting the instrument as he moved it into playing position against his shoulder.

I was seated near the stage, about ten rows back, and even though I had put up with Nap's antics for years, I could not believe that he was actually doing this. Not here, not in front of all these people. Other legislative staffers sat quietly, frozen, unable to move.

Finally, instinctively, I grabbed a walkie-talkie from a colleague and raced onstage. I held the walkie-talkie like a telephone, grabbing Murphy by the back of his collar, and yelling into his ear that he had an emergency phone call. He looked at me, dazed, and I think totally unaware of where he was. I yelled again that he had to come with me, immediately, that an emergency phone call awaited. He grabbed the walkie-talkie, assuming it was a phone, I suppose, but I insisted he would have to place his call in the hotel lobby. That said, I led him offstage and up the steep hill to the Excelsior, where I left him alone in the lobby, confident he could not find his way back to the riverside stage a second time.

I returned to the concert, where the finale had mercifully resumed without a hitch. Afterward, Williams joked about the incident and asked for one favor. "You name it," I said to the exhausted singer.

"You got any more of those Hope watermelons? Man, I love watermelon."

For the remainder of the evening, I sat on the riverbank and watched in amazement as the slender entertainer choked down two huge slices of watermelon, a perfect end to an evening that almost ended in "Great Balls of Fire."

CHAPTER

uch older now and long retired from my legislative career, I look back and realize that the experience with Nap at the concert was a minor thing, but it remains one of my most vivid memories of a unique job that lasted more than twenty-six years. It was also a clear indication of how few people on the legislative staff were risk takers. I was always on the front line in my job, just as the wily Tim Massanelli was in the House. Other staff were buffered, shielded by layers of bureaucracy, and they were always reluctant to offer opinions, take chances, or make tough decisions. I suppose that was good for their job security, but I never respected people who became *furniture*, afraid of their own shadow.

Some people at the capitol didn't like Massanelli for that very reason—his boldness—but I always respected him because he would tell you what he thought, and I tried to do the same thing in my job as the Senate's first chief of staff. After decades there, I learned the hard way that some staff didn't think a whole lot of me, but I understood why, and it never bothered me. The capitol is not unlike other business places—people rise to the top and take their hits, and others who are left behind resent them and become jealous. Before he went to prison, Senator Nick Wilson of Pocahontas told me that if you stay long enough at the capitol, "you're known more by the quality of your enemies rather than the number of your friends." He was absolutely right, and I would learn that lesson in spades years later when a tiny band of misfits tried to oust me from power.

After the incident with ol' Nap that night in 1987, I walked into the office the next day to be roundly cheered by several of my bosses who thanked me for giving Murphy the hook. Senator Paul Benham of Marianna, a likable, albeit brusque, ex-army general, slapped me on the back and told everyone, "By god, whatevvva we payin' you, I'm gonna double it. You got more guts than a guvmut mule."

Benham's pledge for more money didn't materialize, but I appreciated his kind words just the same. But again, giving Nap the heave-ho was not anything in which I took pride; it was just that no one else chose to react to the old rapscallion going onstage. And I had learned a lot about handling people onstage through my years of experience in the *Farkleberry Follies*, a stage show presented by newspaper folk. I had seen my old director, Margaret Carner, remove a rowdy drunk from our audience one evening at Murry's Dinner Theater, and it was a moment that stuck in my mind. I later directed the popular show, and there's no doubt in my mind I drew upon those thespian experiences when it became time to remove Nap from the riverfront venue.

I remember when Marcus Halbrook retired after forty-two years as a legislative employee. He had spent most of that time as director of the Bureau of Legislative Research, the legal arm of the legislature. In the newspaper article about his retirement, the highly revered Halbrook said he was surprised in looking back on his career that he had "survived" so many years at the capitol.

I always remembered that quote, because I think anybody who works a long time inside the Arkansas General Assembly sees himself as a "survivor."

CHAPTER 3

My work at the capitol began on October 15, 1978. State representative John E. Miller of Melbourne, a good-hearted political veteran, was about to take over as Speaker of the House in 1979, and he wanted me to be his new public information officer, a military-type title I detested and later changed. I had worked thirteen years in the newspaper business and was just coming off a two-year stint with Congressman Ray Thornton of Sheridan, who was smarting from a close and crushing defeat in his race for the US Senate.

Ray was an old family friend. His mother, Wilma, a dear, sweet lady, had been one of my favorite teachers at Sheridan High School when I was growing up, and she had taught all my brothers and sisters as well. My three sisters were good friends with Ray, and our Lancaster family was also acquainted with Thornton's uncle Witt, W. R. "Witt" Stephens, brother of Ms. Wilma. I say all this because it was the multimillionaire Stephens, the ultimate Arkansas business/political kingpin, who suggested that I contact John Miller about working in the House of Representatives. Mr. Witt was responsible for leading me to the state capitol years earlier at a time when, still a teenager, I had never been away from home in Sheridan. More about that later.

I telephoned soon-to-be "Mr. Speaker" Miller, and after several meetings, we agreed that I would go onboard as he took over the reins from Representative Jim Shaver of Wynne. I also had support from several other legislators whom I had befriended through the years, namely, Wayne Hampton of Stuttgart and Bennie Ryburn

Jr. of Monticello. I had known Wayne through my work in various conservation movements and Bennie through the Thornton campaign. I also suspected Mr. Witt was on the phone with Miller about my possible employment, and this made me happy and confident. So the deal was struck, and I started to work at the state capitol—never, ever dreaming I would stay so long or, as good friend Halbrook observed upon retirement, "survive" so many years.

My career with the legislature began at an exciting time in Arkansas politics. Bill Clinton had just been elected governor—the youngest in America, he was always proud to say—and he and his long-haired minions were carving up office space on the capitol's second floor about the time I was discussing salary with the House Efficiency Committee on the third floor.

This was the committee that looked after operations and maintenance in the House. In the Senate, this was done by the Efficiency Committee. Being John Miller's new public relations man meant that I had to get the blessing of the ten-member Management Committee, but this was a cinch since Miller was the incoming speaker and a ranking member of the committee; Shaver, a nice, easygoing gentleman, had signed on; and supporters like Hampton and Ryburn were two of the committee's honchos. As I soon learned to say, the issue of my employment was "a done deal."

The committee chairman was W. F. "Bill" Foster of England. I would have written W. F. (Bill) Foster of England, but Foster was insistent that his nickname, *Bill*, be written in quotes and not in parentheses. This was only one of his many little idiosyncrasies—as I soon learned that my new chairman was not only mercurial; he was extremely vain.

It was customary for Foster to handpick a majority of the hundred or so employees who worked during the three-month legislative sessions. Later, when the press started running articles about wives and relatives on the payroll, Foster got scared about the publicity and struck a deal with Howell, the senior senator on the south end of the capitol. Their agreement, known to all insiders, was that Foster's friends, usually people who helped him in his elections, would work off the Senate's session payroll, and Howell would put his friends on the House's session payroll. This way, they could hide most of their patronage people from the press.

Howell was the biggest abuser in this area, placing dozens of friends on the payrolls, including his own children, one of whom worked full-time with the Game and Fish Commission while pulling down a state senate check during the legislative sessions. One Howell favorite, Charles Bussey, a prominent black politician and former Little Rock mayor, stayed on the Senate's payroll for an indefinite period and only showed up on payday. Howell controlled all Senate finances as chairman of the Efficiency Committee and was the person solely responsible for the Senate's multimillion-dollar budget. He often angered young colleagues by not allowing them to see Senate Bill 1, the Senate's biennial funding measure, until opening day of the session. He kept it conveniently hidden away, and any senator who crossed him found himself relegated to a minor committee assignment doled out at Howell's presession Duck Dinner. It wasn't until years later after I arrived as chief of staff that the Senate voted to conduct its first internal audit and hire a well-known independent firm to check on expenditures. The Duck Dinner also went away after Mike Beebe and his new breed insisted that committee selections be made in public, in front of the press. And Senator Nick Wilson embarrassed Howell by having his own chef prepare pan-seared quail, a tasty delicacy, at one of the dinners, allowing diners to choose the quail over Howell's traditional duck dish.

One indication of how Howell hid things in the budget occurred at the start of one session when he unveiled his new Senate Bill 1. It contained a new position for a full-time Senate security officer, and Howell announced to stunned Senate colleagues that the position would be filled by his longtime friend in the state police. But one senator, a relative newcomer, openly challenged the rambunctious Howell and was joined by two other colleagues who threatened to kill the bill. Embarrassed that a young upstart would challenge his authority, Howell passed the bill anyway by a vote of 32-3, only to see the measure hit a wall in the House when highly respected Republican Preston Bynum of Siloam Springs offered an amendment to strike the controversial security position. This set off a war, and Howell, embarrassed over the press coverage, caved in and removed the controversial position. Privately, he seethed for years, annoyed that the House would try to amend his sacred Senate Bill 1. He stood jaw to jaw with the young senator who first challenged him and poked his finger in the senator's chest while vowing revenge.

Senator Knox Nelson, the great facilitator, was the real power in the Senate. Foster was afraid of Nelson's power and catered to him, and Nelson cut Foster in on a lot of the prison legislation that benefited their businesses that sold fuel and other supplies to the Correction Department. Foster and Nelson were in the oil and gasoline business, and it was common knowledge that they made a lot of money off state accounts. It should be noted, however, that this type of arrangement, while controversial, was perfectly legal in those days, long before an ethics law was placed on the books that made such transactions a matter of public disclosure and in violation of certain Senate ethics rules.

The motion to hire me as the House's new information officer was made by Hampton and passed by unanimous vote. It was the first time a committee had ever met to decide my fate, and it was an interesting process to observe. The meeting lasted only a few minutes, and I was warmly welcomed by all my new bosses. The only downside to it all was that my selection meant that another person would be out of a job. That misfortune fell to a young man named Ben, who was very nice to me even after Miller explained to him that I would be his replacement. Ben showed me some of the things he had done in the job, and I always had a nice feeling about him, even after I moved into what had been his office and sat down in what had been his chair.

So it was official. I was now on the public dole. And one of my first tasks was to prepare a press release for Miller and Shaver announcing my selection. I would report to Massanelli, the likable, fiery Italian from Pine Bluff who had worked his way into a permanent job at the House after several years' part-time as the man who operated the microphone system during legislative sessions.

I soon learned about office politics and the deep chasms that existed between certain cliques and employees. The news media always portrayed the legislature as some exclusive club where everyone sticks together, but nothing could have been farther from the truth. There were members who actually despised each other, and there were staff who were resentful and jealous and took sides among the membership. Trust was not something you saw a lot of under the dome, I soon learned, and on some days, the job was like walking in a minefield.

The four women who worked in the House full-time were always at one another's throats. Late one night, at Mr. Witt's Coachman's Inn motel, a celebrated hangout for established politicians and lobbyists, John Miller, Massanelli, and I were discussing the tension between two of the female employees. Finally, Miller broke in and told Massanelli, "At eight in the morning, fire her. She's a troublemaker."

But Massanelli never did fire the woman, and Miller never asked him why he didn't follow through on the order. But the reason was that the employee was a Bill Foster patron, and some of Foster's business sales revolved around her family. In other words, it was politics, pure and simple, and it would have been far too messy between the incoming speaker and his Democratic sidekick Foster. Better just to let it slide, Massanelli wisely decided.

Miller did move to get rid of another employee, though. This secretary was a load from the very beginning of her short and celebrated tenure. She ran into trouble after performing a striptease number at a popular nightclub. One of my friends, a TV reporter, called me at my office and asked me if we had a young blonde who worked in the House. I stopped him short of giving the name and asked him to describe her. I felt like I knew whom he was talking about, and sure as shooting, I did. He informed me that she had caused quite a stir the previous night at the nightclub, taking off virtually all her clothes and dancing topless on a table while screaming that she worked for Speaker John Miller at the Arkansas House of Representatives.

It was hard for me to tell John this, but I knew I had to. He was a very religious man and honestly had a hard time thinking that people actually do things like dance and drink and take off their clothes in front of strangers. But behind closed doors, I had the talk, and in a short time, the stripteasing secretary was history. Those kinds of decisions are rare at the state legislature—members actually biting a bullet and making tough decisions.

It was soon after my first legislative session concluded in 1979 that Foster, while talking with me and several of his colleagues, came up with the nickname that became part of my identity. "You've got the *scoop* on everything," he said in boasting about the good job he said I had done right out of the blocks. And a nickname was born. I became Scoop to my close friends and bosses, and it fit in nicely with others who had similar names. One day at lunch, I dined with Paul "Spook" Berry, Archie "Spike" Schaffer, Cecil "Slick" Alexander, and two well-known Skips—James L. Rutherford III (then with Arkla Gas) and George Holland with Southwestern Bell Telephone. It was hilarious during the meal when one of us would ask for the salt or pepper.

"Hey, Skip, pass the salt to Spook, he told Slick he needed it . . ."

After lunch, we went back to the capitol and had a photo made. The nicknames remained with us, long after our days at the capitol had passed.

CHAPTER 4

As for my "connection" to Mr. Witt Stephens, I'm not sure anyone could call it an actual connection even though I admired the self-made millionaire a great deal and he provided me my first "political" opportunity. I mention him here only because I found it interesting that his name would come up when I met privately with Senator Max Howell about my decision to leave the House in 1985 to become the Senate's first chief of staff.

My first "experience" with Mr. Witt, a fellow Grant Countian, occurred in 1961. He was serving as a member of the House of Representatives, and I was a ninth-grade student at Sheridan High School. I was chosen, because of my good grades, to serve a week as one of Mr. Witt's legislative pages. Back then, the job paid $2 a day, and pages were hired to run errands for the hundred House members. These kids sat on the House floor, and they waited to be summoned by the House members to run small errands around the capitol building.

The $2 a day was pretty good pay for me as a ninth-grader, but the best thing about my weeklong job in Little Rock was my free stay at Mr. Witt's beautiful Coachman's Inn, free meals at the hotel, and a limo ride back and forth to the capitol each day. I was the only page that enjoyed the limo ride, and it was really an eye-opening experience that would last me a lifetime.

Because of this experience, I stayed in touch with Mr. Witt over the years, including my time with Ray Thornton. We shared an occasional private lunch, famous for the corn bread and field peas, and we talked many times by phone. Needless to say, he was a man I deeply admired and respected.

And yes, he did influence John Miller in his decision to hire me in 1978, and apparently, Mr. Witt's involvement meant a great deal to John, who also admired Mr. Witt and had served with Mr. Witt in the House. Apparently, Mr. Witt's phone call to John about me became known to legislators at the capitol because when I went to visit Max Howell in 1985 about the job offer at the Senate, Mr. Witt's name came up very quickly.

"I understand you're a Witt Stephens man," Howell abruptly offered a short time into our visit about the job.

"Well, I think a lot of Mr. Witt," I answered, surprised by his question.

"Well, that's what I'm told, and that's all right," Howell continued as he began to stumble over his words, a nervous habit I would see more of in the coming years.

"Senator Howell, I'll be honest," I continued. "Mr. Witt offered me my first chance to be involved in politics. I was fifteen years old, and I worked as his page in the House in 1961."

"I know that," he said. "But you need to know that Witt's brother, Jack, well, the both of them tried to beat me in one of my first races back around 1946."

I was stunned. I couldn't believe this man, the ranking senator, the ranking lawmaker in the entire legislature, was talking to me about how the Stephens brothers, Witt and Jack, had opposed him in a race thirty-nine years earlier and that I might have some blood on my hands for being a friend.

"Senator Howell, I swear to you that I had nothing to do with that race. I hadn't been born."

"Well, you need to know I won't ever forget it," he said angrily, gritting his teeth.

The memory of that meeting stayed with me forever, and it told me a lot about the man I would soon be dealing with in my new job. The press had frequently called Max Howell a bully, but to this day, I still have trouble coming up with an apt description of the man who I knew resented the day I showed up in my job as the Senate's first chief of staff, a position he was forced to rubber-stamp in order to cajole a cadre of young, impatient Senate colleagues who were moving quickly to take over his long-held fiefdom.

One sidebar about my time as a young page and my five-day stay in Little Rock. I spent those days and nights as Mr. Witt's guest at his Coachman's Inn, a gaslight-lit hotel on property that later became a part of Interstate Thirty and Ninth Street. It was the premier hangout for state politicians, and my experience there was unforgettable. It was the first time I had been away from home in Sheridan, and I enjoyed all the amenities—the beautiful swimming pool surrounded by gaslights, the horse-drawn carriage, and the menu from the Tack Room restaurant that featured items I had never even heard of. My room and meals were free, compliments of Mr. Witt, and I took full advantage, ordering expensive treats such as the turkey breast sandwich, which sold for $2.89.

I also got a free ride to and from the capitol each day in Mr. Witt's personal limo, the only young page to enjoy such luxurious travel. This led to an incident that I kept secret for many years but later opened up about as Mr. Witt and I had a leisurely lunch at his farmhouse ranch in the small Grant County town of Prattsville.

After our meal, the two of us walked out on the front porch. This was in 1979, eighteen years after my ninth-grade vacation from high school to serve as his page. We were sitting on the porch, talking about my new job at the Arkansas House of Representatives, when I mentioned my 1961 experience as his page.

He was kind enough to say he remembered me being one of his pages, but I doubted that he did. I reminded him that one day, while I was there, he summoned me to his desk and told me the House of Representatives would be meeting late into the night, and he suggested I go on back to the Coachman's and call it a day and have supper. He also reached inside his pocket and pulled out a wad of money, thumbing through several hundred-dollar bills until he found a $20. I had never seen a $20 bill, and I certainly had never seen a $100 bill. He gave me the $20 and told me to go outside the capitol's east door and look for the limo driver and, after I got back to the hotel, to split the $20 with the driver.

Then I told him the rest of my story, which I had lived with for nearly twenty years. "I took that $20 bill, Mr. Witt, and instead of walking out the east door and looking for the driver, I went out the west door and walked all the way back to the hotel and kept the whole $20," I confessed.

He chomped on his cigar, smiled, and said, "I always knew you were a smart boy."

I felt a lot better, knowing I had finally exorcised my demon and gotten that off my chest. Maybe my decision as a youngster was an early indication I might have what it takes to head into politics later in adulthood—greed and an affinity for ill-gotten gains.

CHAPTER 5

My theory on politicians is that most are mama's boys and they much prefer to go along to get along. I think history bears this out. Harry Truman said he never made a decision until he checked with his mother. Later examples were Carter, Reagan, Obama, Jim Guy Tucker, Ray Thornton, and on and on. Mike Beebe and Bill Clinton rose to the top and never even knew their fathers, and that speaks awfully well of them both. State legislators certainly are no different. Many are narcissistic and thirst for attention. They always quote their mother in speeches and rarely mention their fathers. Coincidence, perhaps, but my take on this is that most of them are pushed by their mothers to become public servants, ordered more or less to go out and make something of themselves by winning approval from the masses. Whereas dads just kind of kick back and roll with the punches, saying things like "Aw, hell, son, do whatever makes you happy. Runnin' the Shell station sounds good to me."

My unscientific mama's boy theory was never more evident than in the 1977 US Senate race, an event that led me to my eventual career with the legislature. Three good Democrats were vying for John L. McClellan's seat: Governor David Pryor, Congressman Ray Thornton, and Congressman Jim Guy Tucker. Anybody who knew these three also knew their mothers—strong, smart political strategists who I think were instrumental in their sons' decisions to enter politics. Pryor was different in a way in that his father and grandfather were very strong political forces, each serving as popular sheriffs, but his mother also had a taste for politics, becoming the first woman to run for elective office in Arkansas in 1926 in Camden.

But the three mothers' influence became crystal clear to me one Sunday afternoon in Pine Bluff. State Representative Henry Wilkins III, a likable black professor at the University of Arkansas at Pine Bluff, was a strong Thornton backer. He was doing all that he could to help Ray win the US Senate race, and that was becoming an uphill battle in Jefferson County, where Pryor was stronger than garlic.

Wilkins concocted the idea that for Mother's Day, in his big church at Pine Bluff, the congregation would honor Ray's mother, Ms. Wilma, as Mother of the Year. Well, Henry's mistake on this project— like so many he had—was that he had a hard time keeping his mouth shut, especially after a few brewskies at his favorite off-campus pub. To our surprise, he goes to the *Pine Bluff Commercial* with the story that Mrs. Thornton would be honored as Mother of the Year in the upcoming special Sunday ceremony and that the public was invited. The *Pine Bluff Commercial*, at the time, was a well-circulated newspaper, and we knew that a lot of people would read about what Henry was saying, but the whole thing now was out of our control.

Sunday rolled around, and I headed to Pine Bluff with Mrs. Thornton and Ray. We were excited about the plan because we knew this could mean a lot in the black community in terms of election-day support. As we start to take our seats, I glanced to my right, and in the pew directly across the aisle from us were David Pryor's mom and Jim Guy Tucker's mom. Not only did Mrs. Thornton receive her nice award as Mother of the Year, but Willie Maude Tucker and Ms. Suzie Pryor were also feted as Grandmother and Great-Grandmother of the Year, respectively.

It was hilarious, just to see it unravel. All Ray could do was smile and congratulate each of the women. I looked at Wilkins, and he tucked his head with embarrassment. I didn't care about the award and had questioned whether Ray should even appear at the ceremony in the first place, but it was funny to watch all of it unravel in the crowded sanctuary. It was even funnier to watch all the politicians scramble for their pocketbooks when the collection plate was passed around, each one trying to outdo the other. I think the big winner that day was the church's building fund. It isn't often that you end up taking money out of the politician's pocket. Maybe Henry had that in mind the whole time. I wouldn't have put it past him.

To write about my life in politics and omit a chapter about Ray Thornton—well, I would feel like I hadn't written about my life in politics at all. My two years with him on the campaign trail and subsequent encounters helped tremendously in preparing for my eventual career in the state legislature.

You learn a great deal about our magnificent, troubled state in a statewide campaign and from being with a man like Ray. He opened some doors and introduced me to a lot of talented, witty people, many of whom are still very close to me.

One of the most gifted, intelligent, and honest men who had ever served in office—that's Raymond Hoyt Thornton Jr. He was born in Conway, raised in Sheridan, graduated from the University of Arkansas at Fayetteville and Yale, member of the Nixon impeachment committee . . . you see, I still remember all the pertinent stuff in those sophomoric releases.

Ray is living proof that hard work, a good education, and rich relatives can lead to a successful political career. He served two stints in Congress, became president of two major universities, won fame as a crusading state attorney general, and topped it off as a member of the state supreme court—pretty heady stuff for a dorky lawyer named Hoyt, who won acclaim in college as Cowboy Ray.

I could talk straight with Ray—"Sheridan talk," he called it. And I was appreciative that he gave me free rein. But I know I made him angry too, because he told me so years later on the eve of his announcement that he was reentering politics to run for the Second District congressional seat. We were having afternoon coffee at his small apartment at Fowler Square in east Little Rock. He was informing various friends that he would be making the race, and he had asked me for some time to talk things over. As we talked, he said something that I took as the ultimate compliment. "Bill, I used to get so mad at you for saying some of the direct things you said to me, but then I would realize that you were the only one willing to tell me what I needed to hear, rather than what I wanted to hear."

That was probably true, but I simply saw it as having the dirty job of telling my bosses the truth. And I always thought Ray blocked other people out, choosing not to hear criticism. Clinton did that, and I think most politicians have a short attention span, unless the conversation is about them. And some of it is understandable; people who go to see politicians usually are there for one reason and one reason only—they want something.

Years ago, in the late 1970s, conservationists in Southeast Arkansas were fighting special interests in Saline County who wanted to dam the Saline River. The state representative for Sheridan at the time was Gean McDonald, a celebrated hero who had lost a leg in World War II. Gean set up a meeting with then governor Bumpers to tell him that he thought the people in Benton were a bunch of crooks who wanted to dam a scenic river in order to make money off real estate sales. Bumpers, a tenderfoot then, listened patiently and nibbled on a yellow sheet of paper from his legal pad. Finally, he looked at us and said, "You know, the office out there, the waiting room with the secretary, is filled with people every day I'm here, and every one of them wants something. That's all they come here for."

A few other thoughts on that US Senate race—it was a classic, indeed. David Hampton Pryor, Raymond Hoyt Thornton, and Jim Guy Tucker. Ray was the first candidate to use full-color yard signs, and they were expensive. But DeLoss Walker, who had been Dale Bumpers's campaign guru, loved spending Ray's money, and a lot of people valued his opinion. But I will never forget the day Ray called all his campaign staff and volunteers together in downtown Little Rock to introduce the famous consultant. DeLoss, a tall white-haired gentleman who looked like a Hollywood leading man, walked into the room, cleared his throat, and pronounced that we had nothing to fear in trying to defeat David Pryor, that the popular sitting governor from Camden would not even make the cut, and that Ray would defeat Jim Guy Tucker in a runoff. I looked at my friend Paul Berry, and the two of us shook our heads and walked out of the room. I was amazed that we were paying this man a million dollars. "De Lost," I always called him after that.

And then there was the time that two gentlemen from Southeast Arkansas arrived at the headquarters and asked to speak to Ray or one of his lieutenants. The secretary showed them to my office, and they introduced themselves. One was an old holdover from the Faubus days, and he began by promising certain numbers of votes in certain counties. Finally, I said, "So what do you need?" He said he would need $100,000 in cash, small bills, in fact, and he said it without blinking an eye. I told him I appreciated him coming by and that I would meet with Ray. That night, I explained to Ray what had happened. He didn't blink an eye either. "If you hear from them, ask them to come by again, and notify the prosecuting attorney so that he can be here to arrest them." We never heard back.

I was disappointed, of course, that Ray lost, but the day after when he was declared third-place finisher—by a record-close percentage—I hopped into a car with Pryor's people and went to work for them. I liked Pryor, respected him as a person, and was thrilled to help him in whatever little way I could to mop up and move on to the US Senate, where he eventually became our state's most popular elected official. David and Ray had always been friends and remained friends during and after the campaign.

One other sidenote on that campaign. The Pryor-Tucker-Thornton race was very beneficial to Clinton. So many Arkansans, the movers and shakers, were torn between the three candidates in the Senate race. It was hard for a lot of people to choose one over the other because Pryor had been a popular congressman and was the sitting governor; Thornton had been a popular congressman and attorney general and had the backing of uncles Witt and Jack, and Jim Guy was the handsome up-and-comer who had replaced Congressman Wilbur D. Mills.

So who benefited indirectly when the three senatorial candidates came calling? It was Clinton, the young, ambitious gubernatorial candidate and a sure bet to follow Pryor in the governor's chair. Many contributors gave money to Clinton so that they could stay out of the Senate race. The Thornton people heard it every day, and so did the people at the headquarters of Pryor and Tucker.

And who could blame the contributors, heavyweights like bank presidents and leaders of political action committees? They could honestly look friends like Pryor, Tucker, and Thornton in the eye and say, "Gosh, we would like to help you, but we put all our money in the governor's race, you know, Mr. Clinton." So Clinton was reaping this huge windfall, not necessarily because people felt strongly about him, but because they just did not want to take sides in the bigger race. And we all understood that because a thing like that happens a lot in politics.

So Ray got beaten, ended up running an educational consortium, became president of Arkansas State University and the University of Arkansas, and returned to Congress before settling into in a seat at the Arkansas Supreme Court, where he served admirably and honorably until retirement.

I ran into him one day at the big movie theater on University Avenue. He was with his wife, Betty Jo, and he asked for my help in his upcoming race, and I assured him I would always be ready to assist. And then I said, "Ray, you have to be the record holder when you retire. You'll get retirement from being a deputy prosecuting attorney, attorney general, college consortium director, ASU president, U of A president, Congress from two districts, the Supreme Court, and the navy."

He smiled and said, "Leave it to you to think of that."

We laughed and enjoyed the movie.

CHAPTER 6

On the fourth floor of the state capitol, 1978, and it didn't take long to settle into my new digs. Being information director of the Arkansas House of Representatives would become a very enjoyable experience. I had a spacious office above the beautiful House chamber, flexibility as far as time off for lunch, a dozen paid state holidays, and a great working relationship with members of the House and Tim Massanelli.

John Miller was an energetic, cocksure, decisive leader too, a big departure from some previous bosses. A wiry little man with a Barney Fife voice, Miller was at work early and wanted us there with him, and he stayed late, always taking work home. He was a teetotaling Baptist who believed in keeping legislators late in the session. When some of his colleagues were hustling drinks and women at popular bars like Buster's and Tramps, John Miller was ordering more work for people like Massanelli and myself, who were happy to assist.

Miller was also a good sounding board for the young governor on the second floor. Clinton was popular, but it didn't take long for his staff, headed by Rudy Moore and Steve Smith, to piss off a lot of people they came in contact with, including legislators. Throw in Jim McDougal—yes, the one of Whitewater fame—and you had enough arrogance to choke McDougal's wife's horse. (She rode the horse in her TV commercials.)

Their arrogance was certainly more than Representative L. L. "Doc" Bryan of Russellville could handle one day in the governor's office. Doc, a funny, bald-headed ex-radio disc jockey, had become a respected leader in the House. Some Democratic legislators were waiting to see Clinton in the small corridor that ran between the governor's office and the public reception area. There are various accounts of what transpired, but what I remember is seeing Doc becoming furious with Rudy Moore and slamming him against the plywood wall outside Clinton's office. He began choking Rudy and would not let up. Rudy, a small thin man with long hair and a beard, was no match against the muscular Doc, who was a star football player back in earlier days at Arkansas Tech. But soon, order was restored, but Doc threatened Moore, and the threat left Moore visibly shaken.

Legislators like Doc tried from time to time to convince Clinton that some of his staff members were not doing the kind of job that supporters believed to be in the governor's best interest but Clinton and some of his young crowd were pretty impressed with themselves. Julie Baldridge, who gave up a successful career at the *Arkansas Gazette* to work for Clinton as press secretary, was well respected, but some staff were even too much for easygoing and talented Julie. She told me one day that Clinton had surrounded himself with "yes" people who lacked the necessary courage to stand up to him. "All they want to do is touch the hem of his garment," she said in disgust.

CHAPTER 7

The Arkansas House of Representatives is made up of a hundred members. Each member is elected to a two-year term. House and Senate districts are redrawn by the governor, secretary of state, and attorney general every ten years, and they are "gerrymandered," or configured, so that the state is divided equally according to population. When the jigsaw puzzle plan is finalized, each of the hundred districts is made up of about twenty-six thousand people or one-one-hundredth of the state's population. This way, theoretically, each House member represents about the same number of people.

In recent years, population in the northwest corner of the state has soared, while Southeast Arkansas and areas in the Mississippi River Delta have lost population. This population shift has caused a great change in the makeup of the House and Senate and has exacerbated tensions between certain groups, including people like higher-education officials who lobby the legislature for money. Dollars usually flow to the population, and when areas are losing population, it stands to reason that they will lose money for their schools, health centers, and education facilities.

Republicans continue to make gains in the post-term-limits era, but time will tell how successful they become. Certainly, Mike Beebe proved to be one of the state's best governors, the first gubernatorial candidate to carry all seventy-five counties, and successor Asa Hutchinson, a Republican, sailed through his first legislative session in 2015 and generally received high marks.

No doubt, the old axiom about politics being local is true. No one questions this. Most people approve of their own local legislator, but the general public continues to have a very low opinion of lawmaking bodies such as the General Assembly and Congress.

This is easy to understand. Most people don't like politics, and most people don't even bother to vote. Recent legislative races have been won with record-low turnouts. It isn't unusual now for a candidate to win a legislative race with just a few hundred votes. Unheard of years ago, but term limits changed things dramatically and, in my opinion, made local politics less interesting. When veteran politicians remained in power a long time in the House or Senate, they had tremendous name recognition in their local districts, and they were masters at turning out the vote. And people were more interested in politics years ago than they are today in this post-Watergate era when they've seen their leaders, including presidents, lie and cheat and resign in disgrace. Deep down, people don't trust politicians, and it's been this way since biblical days, people resenting the taxing authority. I always thought the person with the ultimate bad title was the tax assessor. How would you like to tell your children that you are the tax assessor? You might as well say you are an ax murderer.

My time in the House lasted from October 1978 to June 1985, about seven years. In that time, I met and worked with some wonderful people—intellectually gifted men and women who were honest and hardworking public servants who loved politics and enjoyed helping people who ran afoul of government red tape.

Stalwarts like Mike Wilson of Jacksonville, Lloyd McCuiston of West Memphis, George Wimberly of Little Rock, and others already mentioned like Bynum and Hampton, Miller and Shaver—they were extraordinary political leaders who did good things for people, regardless of social standing or political persuasion.

Very few problems existed at the House of Representatives, and things ran smoothly as long as there was a competent speaker in charge. There were occasional flare-ups when controversial bills emerged. Abortion was always a huge controversy in the 1970s and '80s when Republican extremists made members vote on hot-button issues they knew were unconstitutional. This was always painful, and privately, Democrats and well-intentioned Republicans fumed over attempts by the radicals to push an agenda for political reasons.

The biggest problem I observed with House members was their imaginary poor self-image and when they compared themselves to their colleagues in the Senate. You could see steam spewing from their ears when the press referred to their chamber as "the lower chamber." Most House members saw senators as arrogant and aloof, while only a few had a close working relationship with the men and women in the "upper chamber." As one astute lobbyist friend described them to me, in nobility terms, "The Senate members are seen as the dukes and the House members, the knights."

Senators, like the mercurial Ben Allen of Little Rock and the explosive Max Howell of Jacksonville, didn't help this situation either. Allen was a pompous elitist and the darling of the *Arkansas Gazette* editorial writers. Time and again, he exhibited defiant behavior on certain issues, and this stoked the flames among fuming House members who embellished tales about Senate dominance. Admittedly, some House veterans cleverly exploited the myth, cradling young House rookies under their arm, telling them that trust was important and that they would protect them from the forces of evil in the Senate.

In one legislative session, Allen refused to allow a House member to present his bill in Allen's Senate committee. Later, the House retaliated and blocked all of Allen's bills from the House floor. Allen, seeing his mistake, broke the stalemate by humbly walking to the north end of the third floor and asking forgiveness in an unprecedented speech before the entire House membership.

And Howell was the personification of evil to some House members. Nelson and Howell were close, but I always suspected that Knox Nelson had a hand in ruining Howell's image with some House members. That way, if House members wanted a favor in the Senate, they would crawl to Knox rather than the senior senator from Jacksonville who had been a fixture at the legislature since 1946. In his long tenure, Nelson, a high school dropout who grew up in Goat Shed, Arkansas, became the most brilliant, calculating, and ruthless politician among the 135 members. He was arguably the most effective state legislator who ever lived, and he rated that top billing status with me too.

Bills were passed in the House once they got the support of the Democratic leadership. Republicans like Preston Bynum and Carolyn Pollan were included in some of the planning, but Republicans were greatly outnumbered then, and Democrats ruled the roost, and everyone accepted that as the norm.

My job was made easy because I had the opportunity to work with some exceptional men who became speakers. Up until Bobby Hogue of Jonesboro changed things and got reelected to back-to-back terms, the Speaker of the House could only serve one two-year term.

Technically, I worked two and a half months under Speaker Jim Shaver of Wynne before my work really began to take off under Speaker John Miller in January of 1979. Shaver was a respected lawyer and came from a distinguished political family, and he was helpful to Miller in the transition as John moved into the big chair.

Following Miller, Lloyd McCuiston moved into the top spot, and after that, I worked under Speaker John Paul Capps—all of them excellent and hardworking Democrats who brought a lot of progressive leadership to the table.

McCuiston had a reputation as being a pawn of special interests in West Memphis, namely, the mob-owned dog track. For years, Bill Ingram had been the state senator from West Memphis and had looked after the dog track's legislative agenda. McCuiston had helped in the House and was helpful to Ingram's son, Kent, in 1983 after Kent took over the Senate seat following his father's death.

McCuiston made no secret of his affection for the track. It would have been political suicide for him not to protect the track when it came to tax breaks. But to his credit, McCuiston never was heavy-handed in his dealings with members and soon became a favorite with his ninety-nine colleagues and many members of the Senate.

McCuiston also was quick to admonish members who steered off course. It happened one day when Lloyd had to leave the speaker's chair to admonish Bill Sanson of Vilonia.

Sanson, an old-machine politician, had enjoyed a long tenure in the House years earlier when kingpins like Orval Faubus, Marlin Hawkins, and Paul Van Dalsen were controlling much of the state's political agenda. After several years in absentia, Sanson had returned to the House, and he was finding out quick that things had changed dramatically.

One of Sanson's first acts was to fashion a bill that would have fired a county employee back in his hometown—a brutal thing, not to mention it would have been entirely unconstitutional. Anyway, word circulated about what was happening, that Sanson reportedly got mad at a man who drove the county's road-grading machine and had prepared a bill to have him fired.

McCuiston had taken the chair as the afternoon session got underway. Sanson, standing at his own chair in the huge chamber, raised his hand and shouted for McCuiston's attention to be recognized, to ask why his bill was not being placed on the calendar for consideration.

McCuiston refused to look in Sanson's direction, and Sanson kept raising his voice. Finally, McCuiston looked down at me—I was seated only a few feet away—and instructed me to ask Sanson to meet him in the speaker's office at once.

McCuiston asked another member to take his place in the big chair and preside over the proceedings, and he asked Massanelli and me to join him in the office. We were there and waiting on Sanson, who burst in and started addressing McCuiston. McCuiston asked me to shut the door, and then he turned on Sanson.

"Listen to me, Bill," he began on Sanson. "Things have changed since you were here before. I didn't recognize [call on] you because that bill you wrote is a piece of crap, and I'm not going to recognize you this entire session. You got that? Now, if you want to go out there and pull that bill down [do away with it] I might reconsider, but don't ever embarrass me or this House again."

Sanson was speechless. McCuiston left him standing alone in the speaker's office, and the three of us walked out. Later that day, Sanson removed his bill from the pending calendar, and it was never brought up again.

McCuiston might have had some faults—too close to some of the machine politics in his area perhaps—but he became an excellent speaker. More outgoing than the workaholic Miller, Lloyd liked to party at night and take his wife, Lib, to some of the nightspots. He enjoyed the social trappings of the office much more than Miller did, and a favorite hangout was the Flaming Arrow Supper Club in the Quapaw Towers, a high-rise apartment complex that was becoming the real powerhouse locale in Arkansas politics.

A favorite McCuiston story, and one that showed how Massanelli and I were often "trapped" in our jobs by being on the front lines, centered on legislative day at the horse races. Before interest in the horse races waned, Oaklawn Park and its lobbyists liked to invite legislators and some staff to a day at the races. It was a nice affair with good food, but it came with a huge price—you had to listen to track owner Charles Cella make a very long speech.

For several years, House and Senate members traveled to the track on a big chartered bus. We were returning from the track after a long day, and the bus pulled into the west parking lot of the capitol. Massanelli and I, looking after McCuiston, stepped off and in the darkness began looking for our fearless leader. He finally stepped off the bus, and a lady passenger who had just met Lloyd reached for his hand and shook it and told him how much she enjoyed meeting him. He thanked her, and as she turned to leave, she leaned over and gave him a small kiss on the cheek.

Well, it surprised Lloyd that she would do that, but he was the kind of guy that people wanted to hug. He was short and funny and, I presume, huggable. The three of us turned to walk away when, to our surprise, Lloyd's wife, Lib, emerged from the large marble staircase. She had driven over from West Memphis and had not made the trip to the racetrack.

"Lloyd, who was that woman that kissed you?" she began, obviously upset over what she had seen.

Never lost for words, McCuiston looked at her and said, "Hell, Lib, I don't know. She's some woman Tim and Bill introduced me to."

Tim and I shook our heads and walked away with Lib and Lloyd, who were laughing along with us.

McCuiston arguably could have been the most popular speaker in modern times. Cecil Alexander of Heber Springs probably held the title until McCuiston's reign, and John Paul Capps of Searcy, who followed McCuiston quickly, became a hit because of his enlightened approach to the office and overwhelming popularity with the news media.

Under Miller, McCuiston, and Capps, the House moved forward in addressing nagging problems such as education and health care. Having Bill Clinton and his wife, Hillary, to articulate the problems helped keep the pressure on. I stayed extremely busy, especially during sessions, and discovered that having a hundred political bosses can be very demanding, to say the least. I did all that I could to help every one of the members and helped change the House's image. And I think we made tremendous progress despite occasional and predictable setbacks. I managed requests from the media, put members into their own radio programs, started a radio program of my own, peddled a dog-and-pony slideshow to civic clubs, and positioned articulate members like Capps and Jodie Mahony of El Dorado on live TV as much as possible.

My only setback occurred when the Arkansas Democrat newspaper got angry with me and launched an investigation into my telephone records. They attacked Massanelli too, and they published articles about phone calls made from my office to my father-in-law and mother-in-law in Malvern.

I finally went to John Miller, and he told me not to worry about the articles. He said the press always hammered on the members and that the attacks on me and Massanelli actually endeared us to the membership. But I went to Miller to explain the real story behind the phone calls to my in-laws, something that remained a secret to most for all my years at the capitol.

My father-in-law was a big fan of the horse races, and he was a close friend of one of my favorite representatives from Conway. The representative, a quiet, ultraconservative Church of Christ deacon, walked to my office every morning to use my phone. He had told me that he was a friend of my father-in-law, and we would talk about this from time to time. What I did not know until the newspaper published my office's phone records was that it was the state representative who was using my phone to call my father-in-law, who, in turn, was placing his bets at the horse track.

And the call to my mother-in-law's flower shop, I explained to Miller, was my call on behalf of Miller to order flowers for Wayne Hampton's mother's funeral.

I explained to Miller that I felt as though I were trapped by the newspaper articles. On the one hand, I could explain that I had not made the calls to my father-in-law, but then I would expose one of my bosses, who was a closet gambler and who would be excommunicated and probably divorced. On the other hand, if I said nothing, I would continue to be abused, and I wasn't in favor of that.

Miller smiled and assured me that the best thing to do was take a bullet for the team and that the controversy would dissolve in time. He was right, and my keeping quiet won me a lot of support among my bosses, who were made aware of the real story. As for the representative who liked the ponies? Well, he became one of my more ardent supporters and couldn't seem to do enough for me. Even today, I think he's still very big in the church.

CHAPTER 8

I moved up quickly in the House. My policy was simple—treat everyone the same while remembering that certain established "leaders" would be more in demand and would be more demanding. I found out that the speaker's time is very valuable, and he is pulled literally in a hundred different directions in the House and many more directions by senators, staff, and the media.

John Miller was also busy traveling the state to discuss a statewide tax initiative, and many times, Massanelli and I had to saddle up and go with him.

My hours were long, but they passed quickly, and it would be hard to explain just how pushed for time I was on certain days. My staff and I often worked all night on Thursdays during legislative sessions because I prided myself in having a long summary report/weekly recap on the members' desks when they arrived on Friday morning. The legislative session adjourned at noon on Friday, and I didn't want the members to have to wait for the report before they left town. In those days, producing a twenty-page typewritten report on all the bills that had passed during the week was extraordinarily demanding because there were no computers, and our production method was cut-and-paste. The members were also given a weekly wrap-up speech and copy for a radio show once they arrived back home.

On nights when I was not at the office, I was learning about the social demands of a legislative session and the legislative nightlife. Miller was taking me places, and then other members wanted me to accompany them too. This was placing an extreme hardship on my homelife, but I felt like I had to be where my bosses wanted me, and honestly, a lot of the outings were enjoyable.

One of the popular hangouts was the Flaming Arrow, a dark, secluded supper club on the first floor of the Quapaw Towers apartment complex at Ninth and Interstate. Several of the House members had apartments in the building, but the main reason this was becoming *the* place in Arkansas politics was because Knox Nelson had an apartment on the top floor, and his comfortable pad had become the legislature's brain center.

Speaker Miller was very close to Nelson, and they would meet there for marathon planning sessions. Young Governor Clinton would meet with them too to listen as Nelson and Miller explained the intricacies of the legislative budgeting process. Downstairs in the supper club, a jazz combo would play favorite tunes while lobbyists bought drinks and dinner for legislators, some of whom were seated with wives and girlfriends.

CHAPTER

On a trip to Colorado, I stopped briefly at Monarch Crest, a mountain retreat that sits atop the great Continental Divide. It is here where the great Rockies actually crest and divide from the plains.

While visiting there in my new job, I made the observation to a colleague that the Arkansas legislature might be reaching its own great divide. More and more progressive legislators were separating themselves from a lot of the obstructionist behavior that had held the state back. There was a feeling that Clinton could actually be the answer to moving the state out of its dismal past.

Clinton's service had been interrupted briefly by Frank White's surprise victory, and after Clinton returned in 1984, he went out of his way to be more accommodating to legislators, almost to a fault. He poured himself into his work, and he offered innovative educational programs that scared the living daylights out of some legislators. But he discarded a lot of the abusive staff from his first administration, and his office was running much more smoothly, thanks in large part to Betsey Wright, who was in charge of office operations, and old pros like Maurice Smith and Bobby Roberts, who were helping lobby lawmakers.

Privately, some legislators seethed over Clinton's agenda, but they couldn't hide the fact that they were liking the young leader more and more. Some House members felt inferior to Clinton—the Rhodes Scholar persona, etc.—and it was uncomfortable for me to sit in small groups in the House quiet room or at a smoky bar and hear some of their disparaging comments about the governor and his wife. But this was typical of some House members: putting on a smiling face when talking to someone and then stabbing them in the back when they weren't looking.

Miller, Capps, Nelson, and others were solidly committed to Clinton and were driving forces behind his initiatives. Mike Beebe, the new senator from Searcy, also was emerging as a positive force for the Democrats along with newcomer Morril Harriman of Van Buren and ever-steady David Malone of Fayetteville.

As Clinton became stronger, so did the Senate. There was a smattering of talent in the House, but the brainpower was impressive and dominating in the Senate. Nelson was in total control of the legislative agenda through brute force and raw politics. And the House was no match intellectually against Beebe, Harriman, and Nick Wilson, who were positioning for leadership roles once Nelson and Howell abdicated.

I tried to focus entirely on my work in the House, but I would run into Nelson, Howell, and Clarence Bell from time to time in legislative meetings and at social functions. Bell was everybody's favorite. A grandfatherly type, the old football coach and superintendent from Parkin in East Arkansas was living a comfortable life as a state senator and a part-time employee at Arkla Gas. He was an old friend of Witt Stephens and had known Mr. Witt when Stephens and his brother, Jack, owned Arkla. Bell had even managed to stay friends with Sheffield Nelson even though the Stephens brothers had disassociated themselves from Nelson after Nelson became president of the gas utility.

When I had the chance to talk with Max Howell and Knox Nelson, they would ask me about my work in the House. They were cunning, and they already knew the answers to most of their questions, but they were feeling me out, and I was all right with their approach.

The Senate had a public relations man, but he was an old Howell patron who, some senators said, never worked, and what time he did show up at the office, he spent on meaningless errands for Howell. Some of the younger members were seeing my handiwork with the media and in speeches I wrote for House members, and they were putting pressure on Howell and Nelson to hire better help in the Senate.

One senator, Veda Sheid of Mountain Home, even went so far as to hijack one of my speeches. The text was being run off on a copier, and Sheid, an elderly woman, snatched it from one of my employees, who tried to put up a struggle. Told by my assistant about what happened, I walked to the Senate and spotted Sheid at her chair in the chamber. I walked up, and she greeted me, enthusiastic about the speech, and I told her that I had come to retrieve the material.

"But I want it, it's mine," she whined.

"No, ma'am, this belongs to the House," I said, removing the paper from her hand.

On three occasions from 1981 through 1983, Howell met privately with me about leaving the House and going to work in the Senate. I didn't tell anyone about the meetings, and I considered each of the offers seriously but eventually turned them down. Most of my work with Howell centered on his annual roast-and-toast in Sherwood. This was a big dinner that raised a lot of money for North Pulaski County charities, and Howell was always nervous about how the roasters would present their remarks.

I was happy to write the program because comedy was something I enjoyed and excelled at, and he knew this. Legislators were very adept at locating talent, and they would tap every available source. But I didn't mind helping the senator, and a lot of the roasters were House members, so the charitable work ingratiated me with my bosses, who would hear from their colleagues in the Senate about how helpful I had been.

But Howell persisted in his efforts to hire me away from the House, offering one time to make my job a joint assignment where I would be information director for both the House and Senate. But I turned away this offer too, explaining to the senator that House and Senate members often were in competition over certain things and that House members often ran against senators, and I didn't want to find myself in the middle of such heated battles.

I was able to recommend two different people that Howell ended up hiring, and I worked with them to show them things that I was doing in the House. My work was going well; I was backed by

Massanelli, who arranged my promotion to information director/ assistant coordinator of legislative services, and I started to travel around the country on some of the famous junkets that the press liked to write about. One trip, strictly business, took me to Mississippi. John Paul Capps was the speaker, and he went with me to explain to the Mississippi House leaders what I had done in Arkansas to publicize legislators. The Mississippians had heard about my programs at a meeting of the Southern Legislative Conference, and their speaker of twenty-eight years, Buddy Newman, was ready to make changes. The Mississippi trip went well, and the House there set up a program like mine and hired their first information director. More than ever, I was feeling good about myself and what I was doing to improve the image of the Arkansas House members.

My biggest obstacle, however, was not the enduring bad image of the legislature. Slowly we were making headway there, thanks to my work with the press and extensive travels around the state. The biggest obstacle was beginning to be the members themselves, some of whom were filled with jealousy and rage.

It had been a snap to talk the media into featuring Capps or Miller or even the flamboyant Lloyd George in feature articles, but the effort was backfiring to an extent as some members who were not so influential began to rebel. One newspaper labeled some of the members "furniture" because they hardly did anything to distinguish themselves in their work.

Grady Arrington of Stephens was one such person. This quiet, easygoing banker who reminded me of Mayberry tax collector Howard Sprague on the old Andy Griffith TV series exploded on me one day on the House floor. He was livid over the fact that Capps and Miller were getting constant attention from the media and that he was going unnoticed.

"John Paul and them are getting all the publicity, and the papers never write about me," Arrington began, his voice quivering and his face turning red. "You're not being fair."

Henry Wilkins III of Pine Bluff said almost the same thing, three days into a new legislative session. "I've been here three days, and they ain't written a thing about me," the House member began. "You gotta do something, Mr. PR Man."

It was frustrating to deal with some of this. It was true I was feeding ideas to the press, but I was not doing anything to favor one member over another. The fact of the matter was that the press had their favorites, people like Miller and George, who were "good copy" and men who were very quotable, and there was very little I could do to encourage reporters to write about people they didn't respect or that they found dull and boring.

I also knew where John Miller and others wanted the publicity ship to sail, and I was doing all I could to weigh a rusty anchor and set a new course to reshape the House's backward image. If this meant scheduling articulate, handsome members like Capps and Mahony for the TV stations ahead of others, I was willing to take the abuse because I had Miller's strong support.

All over Little Rock, legislators were gathering to talk about changing attitudes and what the new, long-haired young governor was proposing. Some members were excluded from the intimate affairs, seen as too obstructionist and old guard. At times, the press would proffer the myth that the legislature was a 135-member club that always stuck together, but nothing could have been farther from the truth. The fact of the matter was that the legislature, from the late '70s into the twenty-first century, was terribly fragmented, divided into warring factions that often hindered progress. More than once, I was seated at restaurants with legislative leaders, and they would actually hide when some of their colleagues walked through the door. They were embarrassed to be seen with them.

And I would learn that there were stark differences between the House and Senate and House and Senate members. The term limits amendment of 1992 gradually reduced the differences because all legislators became limited in the time they could serve. As a result, there was no longevity, no brotherhood, no togetherness, no social club. Before term limits, some House members wound up in the Senate, and their metamorphosis soon occurred as the lengthened term gave them more self-assurance and confidence. It might have been perceived as arrogance—and sometimes it was—but the Senate was the leading force in state politics for a very, very long time. If you wanted laws changed, you best get on board with the Senate. House members, governors, lobbyists, and power brokers knew this.

Sociologists and political scientists may argue that such differences didn't exist, but believe me, when you see it and live it, you learn that huge differences did exist. One reason, it is much easier to get elected to the House. Your district is one-third the size of a Senate district, and a House candidate can put together a coalition much easier in a district with twenty-six thousand people that may be in one county than he can in a Senate district made up of sixty-seven thousand people that may span several counties.

Another way of saying this, and it sounds cruel, is that it is easier to fool a smaller group and win election than it is to spread yourself over a bigger voting pool and gloss over a political agenda. I've seen fire-breathing, segregationist, abortion-hating racists elected to the House in modern times, but not as often to the Senate. Many of the House members I knew were more one-dimensional, limited in their thinking and their political role and scope. Many House members are former county officials who had a limited but sufficient enough power base to get them a win in a House race. This might explain why House members, as a rule, can be limited in their agenda, limited in their viewpoint, less tolerable of others, and a little surlier. I guess you can make the same argument if you compare senators to the governor— that the governor has to be more flexible and tolerant since he runs on a statewide basis. These comparisons certainly make one appreciate the gravity and headaches of the presidency.

This built-in insecurity also makes House members more susceptible to strong, opinionated staff like Massanelli, who became a master at twisting House members around his little finger. The reason was, he was far more intelligent than most of the members and a lot more clever. Some members resented him for it too, but they never could get ahead of him.

I observed that the longer terms allowed senators to stand a little taller and make the tough votes. Seasoned House members quietly used this difference to their advantage. Time after time, session after session, you could see House members passing idiotic legislation, only to have it killed in the Senate. This is not accidental. House members with shorter terms sometimes give in to local constituents who demand new legislation. The House member gets this done in his own chamber and then conveniently sees that the Senate lets it die a slow death, usually in a committee meeting. That is why the tough abortion bills, most of which were clearly unconstitutional, sailed through the House where members were afraid to take a stand, only to hit a wall in the Senate, where tough committees like Public Health or Judiciary always pulled the plug.

And the differences between House and Senate members were obvious to the reporters who worked the legislature. That is why strong House leaders like Miller, Capps, and Mahony stood out like sore thumbs and garnered the lion's share of publicity. And it was why capable columnists telephoned senators like Mike Beebe and Morril Harriman when they needed accurate information.

A great line from Little Rock's *Farkleberry Follies*, the popular stage production/political spoof, accurately defined the differences between senators and representatives through one of its characters, who said, "The Arkansas Senate is like a fine bottle of Montrachet while the House is like a pitcher of Miller Lite, warmmm Miller Lite."

Long after he left the House because of term limits, the distinguished Ernest Cunningham of Helena confided in me that it broke his heart to see House members walking the halls of the capitol building in blue jeans. Cunningham, an articulate gentleman who dressed well, had served more than twenty years in the House, had become speaker, and went on to a lucrative business as a lobbyist. He was a traditionalist, and he believed in traditional Southern values. He thought legislators should wear a coat and tie and at least look respectable. Capps, McCuiston, and other House leaders fit the same mold. That is why it was detestable to them when House members wore wild polyester suits or faded jeans to the capitol. It was also another reason senators stood out, because they dressed better and at least tried to look important.

Representative Lloyd George of Danville poked fun at the unofficial dress code by wearing faded overalls on the closing day of the legislative sessions. He said the "overhauls" signified that legislators were country hicks. George was a brilliant, educated man, and the sideshow was fun, but it did lend credence to the popular notion that Arkansas legislators were a bunch of country bumpkins. It didn't help, either, that Nap Murphy dressed like Colonel Sanders on the closing day. He and George together made quite a snapshot for the evening news.

The fun and games almost went too far in 1983 when a CBS news crew out of Atlanta barreled into the House to film on closing day. Jonie Anderson of the local CBS affiliate was a friend of mine, and she telephoned me to say the national news crew was on its way to the capitol. I rushed from my office to tell Speaker McCuiston, who was in his office. He looked at me and said, "Oh my god, Nap's in the chair." This meant that Nap Murphy, dressed as Colonel Sanders, was in the speaker's chair and presiding over the House, and Lloyd George was parading around in his faded overalls. What in the world would CBS think if they walked in and saw this? The speaker and I beat it out to the chamber, pulled Nap from the big chair, and rushed him into a back room just as the film crew walked in.

This was a close call, but so was the arrow-through-the-head episode with the comical Frank Willems, representative from Paris. To show his disgust over a bill, Willems rose from his House seat on the back row to address the speaker and put on a hat that had a long arrow through its center. It made it appear the arrow was poking through Frank's head. He was not aware that a national film crew was in attendance from NBC News in New York. They turned on their camera and filmed away as Frank guffawed and growled about the legislation. Late in the day, I was summoned by the House leadership to see about what we could do to repair the damage, certain to air in an hour on Tom Brokaw's show. I telephoned David Jones, manager of KARK channel 4, the local NBC affiliate. I explained to him what had happened and asked him because of our family ties from growing up in Sheridan if he could look into this. At that time, channel 4 was one of NBC's top-rated affiliates, and Jones had a lot of stroke with the New York bosses. Jones went to work and called back in less than an hour with a promise from New York that the footage would not be aired. My bosses were delighted by the news, and the work was another huge feather in my cap.

Willems thanked me privately, but I'm not sure he was ever aware of how his stunts hurt him and hurt the image of the House. He could be generous and kindhearted, but he also could show a different side to his character. I saw that side one day in the speaker's office.

Speaker McCuiston had asked Massanelli to arrange for lunch in the speaker's office on Monday. The big boss wanted to invite a handful of folks in to eat and discuss the upcoming week of work. Massanelli asked Representative Tom Collier of Newport to pick up some barbecue from one of his friends in the Newport area and take it to the speaker's office. He gave Collier the money, and Collier said he would have the food in the speaker's office at noon on Monday. Monday rolled around, I got a call to go to the speaker's office to eat, and McCuiston shut the door behind me and five others as we prepared to eat. Massanelli knelt down and began slicing the meat and handed McCuiston a plate. About that time, the door opened, and it was Willems. McCuiston didn't want him to go in, but he felt trapped and said, "Come on in, Frank, and get you some food."

Seeing Massanelli in the kneeling position, Willems snapped, "I will, Lloyd, as soon as the damn hired help gets out of the way."

Massanelli, known back then for his temper, jumped to his feet and confronted Willems. "The damned hired help bought the food, Frank."

McCuiston then joined in, "If you wanna eat, Frank, sit down and eat, but you need to keep your mouth shut." He stayed and ate, of course, never one to turn down a free meal.

One of the worst days and saddest days of my career also involved McCuiston and Massanelli. Bill Thompson of Marked Tree was a longtime state representative and very good friend to McCuiston. Uncle Billy, as we knew him, had been a fixture in Arkansas politics for decades and had risen to number 1 in seniority in the House. McCuiston got a phone call from Thompson's sweet wife one day, and she said Bill had not been heard from for a couple of days and that she was worried. He liked to drink and would go on binges occasionally, so Lloyd summoned Massanelli and me.

Our plan was to start our search at Thompson's Capitol Hill apartment across the street from the main capitol building. Thompson occupied a small room on the top floor. The three of us walked outside, and Massanelli noticed immediately that the light was on in the apartment across the street. We walked quickly and took the elevator to the top floor. We beat on the door, but there was no answer. Finally, Massanelli put his strong shoulder to the door, and it popped open. Lying between the refrigerator and the kitchen table was Uncle Billy, with the telephone up to his ear. He had been dead for several hours. It was the end of an era in the Arkansas House of Representatives and the close of a very sad day.

To show you the heartless side of the place, I only have to recall what happened in the wake of the man's death. News spread quickly, and news reports flashed on TV and radio that Thompson had been found dead. By late afternoon, virtually all the House members had received the news, and by six o'clock that evening, Massanelli and his staff had received phone calls from almost all the members. Most expressed their condolences, but three House members called only to ask who would be next in line to claim Thompson's apartment space.

One other story, well, perhaps two, was about Vada Sheid, the senator from Mountain Home. John Miller was the representative from her area of the state. He carried a much bigger stick in the legislature, and it was hard for John to deal with Sheid, whom he considered a lightweight and a sure vote for Senator Ben Allen whenever Allen wanted a yes vote for one of his bills.

We were in the middle of a legislative workday in the House when we received word from the weather bureau that a tornado had been sighted between Benton and Little Rock. The weather alert said the twister was making a beeline for the state capitol and that all the people there should take cover.

Miller summoned me and Massanelli and asked if he should recess the House until the storm had passed. We told him it might be a good idea, and legislators were advised to take cover in the basement of the building, where the cafeteria was located. Miller asked me if I intended to go downstairs, and I told him I wasn't too worried about the approaching storm.

"So you're gonna ride it out up here?" Miller asked me.

"Yep," I said, "I figure the building has been here a hundred years, and I'll take my chances."

"I will too," he said with a grin, shuffling the stack of papers on his desk that needed attention.

"Besides," I added, "I figure your friend Vada Sheid is down there in the cafeteria, and if a tornado hits the capitol, I don't want to die with Vada Sheid lying on top of me."

I thought John would bust a gut laughing. "That would be bad, wouldn't it?" he said.

One other John Miller-Vada Sheid story. For some reason, the House and Senate thought it might be a good thing to pack up and hold an afternoon meeting of the legislature at historic Old Washington in Southwest Arkansas. So we loaded up 135 legislators and dozens of staff to head down to the old state capitol site for a day's business.

Speaker Miller decided he'd drive his car rather than board one of the big buses, so he asked me and Massanelli to ride with him. The business was completed, and it was time to head back to Little Rock. We were about to leave when Miller told me to hurry and get to his car, which was parked out back.

"What's the rush?" I asked him, trying to grab for my coat and briefcase.

"Just hurry," he says. "Vada Sheid said she wanted to ride back with us, and I don't want her to see my car."

Massanelli, Miller, and I jumped into the car and streaked out of the little town, careful not to look back. I was never sure whether Vada Sheid ended up on one of the buses or had to make other arrangements to get back to Little Rock. All I did know was that John Miller was not going to make room for her in his Chevy Caprice.

CHAPTER 10

A few months into the 1985 legislative session, Mike Beebe and Morril Harriman were making themselves heard in the Senate. Beebe, elected in 1983, was thirty-eight years old and already had one session under his belt. Harriman, thirty-four, was a new kid on the block but was beginning to bond with fellow Democratic lawyer Beebe and others interested in good government.

In his first few months at the Senate, Harriman had seen Nick Wilson go a-courtin'. Wilson was becoming uneasy, seeing his influence decline in a political body that was changing dramatically in terms of political ideology. Words like "good government" were being tossed around a little too frequently to Nick's liking, and he was finding himself with fewer and fewer allies.

Ol' Nick, as the press called him, was only forty-two years of age, but he was seeing a power shift in the Senate, and he knew it favored Beebe, who was closely aligned with Clinton. Also, Jay Bradford of Pine Bluff and Wilson's nemesis, Stanley Russ of Conway, were also becoming popular with the news media.

Knox Nelson and Max Howell were caught in middle of the whirlpool of reform, not really knowing where to land. The two dinosaurs knew they were capable of holding on to their power, but they were worried, and they were trying to dilute some of Beebe's and Wilson's strengths by playing the two young leaders against each other.

By dividing them and keeping them apart, Nelson and Howell knew they had a better chance of maintaining their power base. If Beebe and Wilson were to ever team up, like Wilson and Bill

Walmsley of Batesville had done earlier, the power shift would be Richter-scale proportions and doom the two old pros. That is why in their conversations, Nelson and Howell would cleverly say things to Beebe that disparaged Wilson while ambushing the unsuspecting and inexperienced Beebe in talks with Wilson.

Beebe had won his Senate seat without opposition, and he was moving quickly up the credibility ladder with colleagues. By day, the senators worked hard for Clinton, who had turned to veterans John Miller and Knox Nelson and younger minions like Beebe, Bradford, Harriman, and Cliff Hoofman. At night, the social outings were well attended, but there was a noticeable decline in interest as legislators moved away from large gatherings in favor of small dinners with friends and associates who shared their progressive beliefs.

House members were prone to go anywhere there was free food and drinks. Afterward, they would play card games like pitch while stopping by popular nightspots. Senators were moving in a different direction, however. Wilson would hole up with favorite lobbyists at his large apartment at the Capitol Hill building near the Capitol, while Beebe and his growing group of followers were cloistered at a favorite restaurant or hotel room, where they sipped wine and played bridge. Wilson would later label Beebe's group "the Young Golfers," trying to take some of their shine away with derogatory and disparaging statements to his admiring faithful.

There were still some members, House and Senate, who loved the nightlife and would party every night at Tramps or the Wine Cellar or Bobbisox. It was amazing to watch some of them staying out all hours and then appearing magically the next morning at committee meetings, fresh and alert and ready to do the people's business before heading back into the boozy breach again at sunset.

An astute political staffer once observed that the "greatest aphrodisiac known to mankind is the convening of the Arkansas legislature." Truer words were never spoken about some of these men, but things were slowly changing. Some married legislators had girlfriends, and some married female legislators had boyfriends. Most tried to hide their indiscretions, but some acted as though they were invisible, showing up at public functions with jailbait groupies who made no secret of their affection. The reporters knew about it too, but this was a time long before sexual dalliances became journalistic fodder. For the most part, the romantic attachments were not considered newsworthy, and some reporters who had ethical demons of their own would have found it a bit hypocritical to put such matters in the newspaper.

Later, in the new, twenty-first century, there were rumors that two of the male legislators were homosexual lovers and shared a cozy love nest apartment in the shadow of the capitol building. But it wasn't discussed much, and nobody ever came out of any kind of closet. One story kept alive for years by members of the capitol police concerned one of our better-known constitutional officers. The story was that the man and one of his male employees were "caught" in a compromising position in the officer's main office. A female member of the man's staff walked in on the two men and, because of what she observed, abruptly resigned her high-paying position the following day and moved out of state. Some said she moved away because she and the constitutional officer were involved romantically, but another story was that the constitutional officer sent her away and paid her a huge sum of money to buy her silence about what she had seen.

The nightlife, especially during legislative sessions, could be grueling. Most legislators are from out of town; they are invited to social events every night, and alcohol can be prevalent. I did watch as the Little Rock nightlife took a dramatic toll on one young House member. He was a Pentecostal preacher, married, and a father, who became a very outspoken politician early in his career. He ranted against politicians like Clinton and against issues like abortion. He loved seeing his name in print, but he was becoming an embarrassment, even to members of his own party.

But like so many politicians, he preached one thing and practiced another. In the daytime, he would walk to the well of the House and dress down colleagues on whatever moral issue seemed to be on his mind while trashing Clinton's social programs. But by night, he changed into an entirely different creature, a John Travolta wannabe who openly walked into bars with women to boogie down and dance the night away.

The legislator managed to hide all this from his wife, who rarely came to Little Rock, but one member of the media, a well-known anchorman who had been my friend for years, finally got his fill of the Republican's hypocrisy.

"Lancaster, I want you to do something for me," my TV friend began as we talked in my office at the House of Representatives. "You tell your goddamn sanctimonious Pentecostal preacher/legislator that if I see him again at the Capital Hotel, drinking and associating with his hookers, I will have his ass as the lead story on the six o'clock news."

He went on to explain that he was present when the legislator left the hotel the night before with a drink in his hand and in the company of three prostitutes.

I thanked my friend and told him I would have a talk with the person. I walked directly from my office and asked the member to accompany me to an area outside the House chamber. Dozens of people were standing in the crowded hallway as I began to whisper.

"I want you to listen to me, and you're not going to like this. A TV reporter just left my office. He said you left the Capital Hotel last night with a drink in your hand and in the company of three hookers and that if you do something like this again or continue to flaunt this type behavior, he will have you on the news."

I thought the man would die. His face became ashen; his mouth dropped open. He searched for words. "I will not be threatened by some member of the press. I want you—"

"Listen," I interrupted. "Did you do what he said? Were you at the Capital Hotel, and did you leave there with three women?"

"Well, yeah, but I thought they worked for the TV stations."

"That dog won't hunt, and you know it. You can't have it both ways. Little Rock is a little town, and you can't have this both ways."

His head dropped, and he walked away.

Later in the day, he went to my office. "I appreciate you talking to me. I know that wasn't easy. I will not embarrass you or myself again like that."

I appreciated him taking the time to visit with me like he did. We became pretty good friends, and over time, he became a much better legislator.

CHAPTER 11

Every fisherman knows that if you throw chum in the water, you'll see an immediate feeding frenzy. I found out in my years at the capitol that the same reaction occurs when you mention *free* to a member of the House of Representatives. I was constantly amazed at how these men and women responded when there was an offering of free food or other gifts from lobbyists.

As John Miller prepared to ascend to the speaker's job in 1979, he confided in me and Massanelli that he was uncertain about what to do about what we called "the social calendar."

These were the planned social events for legislators during the legislative session and certain other outings when the lawmakers were not in session. Miller, who didn't drink, was straight up in saying he wanted no part in the planning of social events since booze was such a prominent part of the nightly outings. But he did not want to stand in the way of others who wanted to gather at the bars and restaurants, which at that time were offering three-for-one drinks in the afternoon happy hours. Hundreds of lunches, dinners, and watering-hole events were crammed into the sixty-day legislative sessions, paid for by lobbyists, and the planning was an arduous task, to say the least.

Miller decided an easy way to keep him and the speaker's office out of the social planning loop was—what else?—create a new legislative committee. Voilà! The House Affairs Committee was born, and the obvious choice to head up the new five-member panel was none other than Representative J. Sturgis Miller of Pine Bluff, no relation to the new speaker from Melbourne.

Sturgis never saw a lobbyist he didn't like, or cling to, or take money from, or well, you get the idea. When some of the lobbyists heard that Sturgis would become the go-to guy on social events, they promptly started doubling their budgets for food and whiskey. To illustrate Sturgis's penchant for freebies, I'll recite two stories that I think best sum him up.

The University of Central Arkansas had won a national collegiate football championship, and the Conway team and their coach were invited to the House for a celebratory pat on the back. As the team's coach finished his remarks, he apologized for not bringing along some kind of memento to present to the House members. He then held up a small key chain shaped like a bear, the team mascot, and said, "I do have this one little key chain if anybody would like it."

We all laughed at what we thought was a little joke, but Sturgis Miller, ever ready to pounce when a free gift was mentioned, literally climbed over his desk on the front row of the House chamber and snatched the key chain from the coach's uplifted paw. I couldn't believe my eyes, yet we knew if anybody would react so atrociously, it would be Sturgis. It was the most awesome exhibition of greed I'd ever seen, even by his standards—this elderly man leaping over a four-foot-high desk to retrieve the inexpensive trinket.

Later, after the team had departed, Helen Sweezy, a nice lady who had worked as the speaker's secretary for many years, stopped me in the hallway. "Did you see what Sturgis did today?" she said, shaking her head in disgust. "I've seen a lot here, but never anything like that."

But Sturgis was never one to take a step backward. He topped even that performance several years later as we were preparing for the 1987 Southern Legislative Conference mentioned earlier, the one featuring Nap Murphy's unexpected stage appearance.

The planning committee was meeting at the capitol, and we were late getting started as Stuart Bell, our planning expert, explained that Sturgis Miller, the House chairman, was running a few minutes late.

Finally, Miller walked in or, should I say, limped in. He could barely raise his head and was stooped over as he walked. Someone asked what was wrong, and what he said sent all of us into shock. He said he had left a legislative convention in Tennessee when he noticed a display booth set up by a lobbyist from the Eveready battery company. The lobbyist was taking down his display, which featured free flashlight batteries. Sturgis said he asked the man if he could carry some of the freebies back home to Arkansas, and the man said that he surely could. So what did Sturgis do? He said he went to his car, unloaded all his clothes, returned to the conference center, and filled both of his suitcases with the free batteries. As he walked back to the car with the loaded-down suitcases, his back snapped out of place, making it almost impossible for him to walk.

Horrified over what she had heard, Bell looked at Miller and said, "My god, Sturgis, I don't think I would have told that!"

Years later, while in my job at the Senate, I received a phone call late one afternoon. It was from a House member who was calling to ask a favor. He was aware the Senate kept a large stash of canned soft drinks in the Senate Quiet Room. The soft drink lobbying group provided the refreshments free of charge, and it was one of my responsibilities to make sure more drinks were picked up each month and placed in storage. Senators availed themselves to the free drinks occasionally, and House members who went over from their chamber to visit in the Senate lounge were also welcome to share in the free drinks.

This day, the House member was calling because he wanted some of the free soft drinks for his own use—to use in his private apartment across the street in the Capitol Hill building. At first, I thought the call might be a joke, that the House member was just pulling my leg, but it took me only a few seconds to realize he was really serious in his request.

"Are you kidding me?" I said to him, almost wanting to laugh into the telephone receiver.

"Well, nobody has to know," he answered. "I'll come over and get 'em."

"If you need a few Cokes for a party, I can see helping you out, but how many are we talking about?" I asked him.

"Oh, how about seven or eight cases?" he answered.

"Man, I think you better go shopping somewhere else," I told him, trying to laugh my way out of a situation that was becoming very uncomfortable.

We ended the conversation, but the House member never talked to me again, and he always looked the other way when we encountered each other. He left a few years later, a victim of term limits, but he left in style. By that, I mean, one of the capitol policemen told me that the man, on his last day at the capitol, talked the secretary of state into giving him several hundred "free" American flags to carry back home to North Arkansas. He did leave in style, loaded down with government freebies, compliments of the Arkansas taxpayer.

CHAPTER 12

In the spring of 1985, the eightieth regular session of the General Assembly was winding down when I dropped by the Flaming Arrow to meet Massanelli and some House members for dinner. A large group had gathered, and among them was Senator Mike Beebe. I had met him at various social functions and had watched him in meetings at the capitol, but I had never spent time with this new senator socially.

I was seated next to him, and he spent a lot of his time fidgeting with his pipe, unstopping it, putting in fresh tobacco—all the things that pipe smokers do to practice their time-consuming habit.

We talked the usual talk, and then he mentioned the House staff and the things I did in my job. He said people in the legislature had taken notice of innovative things being done in the House and that the Senate wanted to do a better job with its staffing.

I talked about some of the things that I had done for senators, some of them on the sly, and he said he was aware of these things because Nelson, Howell, and Senator Joe Ray of Havana had been singing my praises.

"How would you feel about doing those things in the Senate?" he asked.

I told him Howell had tried a few times to lure me to the south end of the building, but that I was happy doing my job in the House.

"We'll pay you more, and you can select your own staff," Beebe continued.

I was deeply flattered by the overture, and I wondered if he had been sent by Howell and Nelson to make me an offer. I would learn later that it was the group of young senators, not the old-timers, who wanted staff improvements. At that time, the Senate had only a secretary—an elderly Howell disciple—and a young public relations man whom I had recruited for Howell. There were no other staff, and I would soon learn why—Howell didn't want other staff. The senior senator, who had been elected to the General Assembly in 1946 (the year I was born), had enjoyed things his way for a very long time at the Senate. He had a lucrative law practice in downtown Little Rock, supported by numerous state contracts and a fleet of lawyers and secret friends who controlled the legislative agenda. He did not want change, although he told me privately many times that he would enjoy my going to the Senate from the House.

I left the Flaming Arrow that night puffed up. I had enjoyed the conversation with Beebe, but I didn't think I would have an interest in leaving the House of Representatives. I drove home and went to sleep, not sure that I would even give the matter much thought the next day.

But driving to work the next morning, I did, indeed, start to think about the offer. I was thirty-nine years old, had worked at the House about six years, and I had a sincere interest in "good government," thinking honestly and rather innocently that I could make a "big" difference in politics. My nature was to be positive and upbeat, and well, maybe being the Senate's very first chief of staff wouldn't be such a bad thing after all.

Two days later, Massanelli and I went to lunch, and on the way back to the capitol, I asked him to pull his car into the parking lot so that we could talk. He knew what was coming because he was an insider and roommate of the powerful Knox Nelson. He and Knox, longtime Pine Bluff buddies, had no secrets.

I told my friend about the Senate's offer. I honestly think Tim was hurt that I wanted to leave, but I also knew him to be a man who "tells it like it is," and he offered me his best advice. "Scoop," he began, calling me by the nickname given me by Representative Bill Foster, "if there's anybody who can make that bunch happy, it's probably you."

Massanelli was very savvy. He knew the game and played it well. I think a part of him worried that the Senate would devour me, that the self-motivated factions would eat me alive, and he was absolutely right to think that way. But he also loved his work and loved the General Assembly, and I think a part of him wanted the Senate to become better.

The news spread quickly. Word that I might be leaving reached the House chamber. Representative Bruce Hawkins of Morrilton, a fiery Democrat and close friend, went to my office. "I've got a resolution with seventy-nine sponsors telling the Senate to leave you alone. You ain't going over there."

In my calmest voice, I began with Bruce. "Hey, please don't run this resolution [pass it]. I think I want to go, Bruce."

He appeared devastated.

Several of the House members came to visit with me privately after news of the job offer hit the newspapers. Beebe and other senators had started to go over to the House to explain that they wanted me to help the "overall" situation with the General Assembly and that, by having me on the south end of the third floor and Massanelli on the north end, we could all work together better. I don't write this out of ego today—this was the way it was.

G. W. "Buddy" Turner of Pine Bluff, a longtime representative and former speaker, said as much in many of his conversations with me and Massanelli. He would put his arm around the two of us and say to people, "We don't have to worry about the capitol, we've got a Pine Bluff Italian on the north end taking care of the House and a good ol' Sheridan boy on the south end taking care of the Senate." Buddy liked having two of his close friends in charge, especially since they were from his neck of the woods.

After Hawkins pulled down his resolution, he graciously patted me on the knee and wished me well. I left my office and walked to the south end of the third floor of the capitol and asked a secretary for a few minutes with Senator Howell. He heard me outside his office and walked out and asked me to go in.

"You coming?" he asked politely. "We need you."

It was then that I began my first serious conversation with the man I would, over time, grow to always keep at arm's length.

CHAPTER 13

N ames such as Fagan, Nelson, Bell, Bearden, and Jones readily come to mind when political animals discuss some of the earlier colorful history of the Arkansas Senate. And by earlier, we're talking 1940s-'70s. Other names, such as Wilson and Beebe, would follow before term limits wiped out any chance of subsequent institutional memory or history.

I remember a song from the 1973 *Farkleberry Follies* stage show that named some of the more famous legislators, a song written to the tune of "Yellow Rose of Texas." The words were "The legislature runs this state,/that ain't no fairy tale,/if there is one thing that we hate,/it's pushy guys like Dale [Bumpers]./We've got Bubba Wade and Linder,/Doc Bryan and Clarence Bell,/if you can't respect such splendor,/you can just go straight to hell."

Many of the legislative names before term limits did become familiar, and some were legendary in Arkansas political history. A senator asked me once why I thought people remembered certain legislators, and I told him I thought it was because certain legislators emerged as leaders and the newspapers in Little Rock, because they had statewide distribution, made them famous. And certain names had a magical ring to them—Nick Wilson of Pocahontas, Clarence Bell of Parkin, Mutt Jones of Conway . . . Robert Harvey of Swifton.

But William Max Howell of Jacksonville had to rank at the top of the class as far as legislators who ruled the roost in terms of raw, unadulterated power. He became furious with me soon after I took the job in the Senate when my brother Bob, a newspaper columnist, named the three biggest bullies in politics, and his selections were (1) Max Howell, (2) Max Howell, and (3) Max Howell.

When he visited with me about working for the Senate, he let it be known that he kept an enemies list and that he never ever forgot or forgave a person who worked against him. This was when Witt and Jack Stephens were mentioned, but he eventually went in another direction, which was his nature. Howell was good at running his bluff, like a poker player who sizes up a competitor, and then smiling nervously, grinding his teeth, and moving on to another subject. Some of the time, he would tell people "I love ya" and then laugh nervously. Years later at a roast-and-toast dinner, Senator Travis Miles of Fort Smith, a nice, easygoing man, roasted Max and said, "When Max says 'I love ya,' you better reach for the Vaseline because you're fixin' to get screwed."

After dealing with Howell for several years, Senator Charlie Cole Chaffin of Benton described Howell as "a playground bully." She said, "You remember the bully back in grade school, how he would come up and stand in your face. Max does that, especially to me because I'm a woman. But you know what you have to do. You have to punch a bully right in the damned face, and then he'll leave you alone."

In that first meeting, Howell talked briefly about the factions in the Senate, how he would clear my pending employment with the five-member Efficiency Committee, and what my pay would be. We parted company amiably, and I walked back to the House of Representatives to resume my work for the day.

I went to work in the Senate in June 1985. Howell had suggested I hire a woman who worked for the Legislative Council, a close friend of his, as my assistant, but I chose not to do so because Beebe and some of the younger senators didn't like that choice. It pissed off Howell and probably set the tone for some of our ensuing troubles, but he never let on publicly about my decision.

I hired a young man named William Parks to be what we called the properties officer. This included some basic janitorial services, but his work involved a lot more than that—taking care of all the offices, furniture, the huge chamber where the senators voted on bills, etc. Parks was recommended to me by Allen Gordon, a young senator from

Morrilton, and my first recruit was very appreciative of the chance to work at the capitol and leave his dead-end job at a Morrilton liquor store.

Slowly but surely, I put the team together, and the senators began to see an immediate change. Beebe was careful about it all, massaging Howell at every turn to make him understand that none of the change would have been possible without him. It was a silly game we had to play but a necessary one.

Nelson warmed up to me slowly and would call me frequently from his Pine Bluff business. He would always get his digs in at Howell and anyone else that was annoying him at the time, but Nelson was crafty and conniving, and I listened to him.

I was beginning to learn the real art of politics. The people at the various state universities who taught politics and the newspaper columnists who wrote about the inner workings at the capitol—well, I soon learned they didn't know how the real game is played. They didn't have a clue as to what it was really like, dealing every day with an egomaniac or an insecure power broker or young tacticians like Beebe and Wilson and still pretending everybody was on the same team. It was a hell of a position to be in, "an impossible job" trying to please thirty-five politicians, Knox Nelson later would say to me.

I could write the rest of this book about Max Howell, my trials and tribulations with this seasoned warrior, but let me begin by simply saying that I never could make myself put my total trust in him. No one I knew at the capitol did, and I think that was because Max Howell didn't fully trust anyone else in politics probably because he had been lied to a lot over his forty-year career. I watched him berate state employees, lobbyists, colleagues, and longtime friends. He fired a legendary employee on the Senate floor one day, poking him in the chest madly and saying, "You've lied to me for the last time." And this because the veteran servant had simply suggested a roll call on a bill when Howell didn't want one.

Governor Bill Clinton said of Howell, "He just wants to be treated like every other Roman emperor."

David Pryor said one of his worst days as governor was when he had to veto three of Howell's bills and incur the senator's ensuing rage and wrath.

The capitol complex installed a new phone system in the mid-1980s. We heard that Nelson had a hand in the bidding process, but there was no criminal trail to it. I didn't think anything about the Senate getting new phones until a new phone showed up at my desk one afternoon, and the installer said he would need some time into the night to finish the work. Trusting and innocent soul that I was at the time, I left and returned the next morning. The new unit in my office had a blinking red light to signify that someone had left a message. To my surprise, the light was blinking, and I had never even used the phone. I punched the button next to the blinking light, and a man on the other end of the phone answered, "Police department, can I help you?"

A cold shiver went up my spine. I hung up quickly without talking. It was my first feeling of paranoia, but my first thought was that my phone had been tapped, and the installer had tested his handiwork by calling his bosses at some police department. I had no way of knowing this for sure, but I suspected from that very moment on that someone friendly to someone in a position of power in the Senate would now be listening in on all my conversations. Who, I didn't know for sure, but my mind was spinning with suspicion and a large helping of fear.

Over time, I didn't know how I learned to play along, but I did. Suspecting my phone was tapped—that was about as spooky a thing as I ever went through—I could imagine all sorts of bad things ahead, but I used it to my advantage, telling no one. If certain people were listening in, I would try to turn the tables.

Every one of my phone calls from my office, for years, would be carefully planned. I would watch every single word I said. You can imagine how difficult this was, but I did it. If I wanted to make a personal call, I'd use one of the phones in the Senate Quiet Room, far removed from my office.

In my conversations with senators, I would steer callers away from anything controversial. Senator Beebe, my most frequent caller, would always laugh and ask, "How's ol' Max?" and I would respond, "Senator Howell seems to be doing fine."

Some conversations were vague and total bullshit, but I was playing the game and wondering if someone, some senator, some   ·

policeman, really might be listening to tapes of me. I didn't want to believe it, but I had to make myself understand some people's surreptitious capabilities. It was not on the scale of White House ordered break-ins, but I had to face some very hard facts. I certainly couldn't turn to the authorities—the man who answered the message machine was sitting at a police department, obviously breaking the law and working on someone's secret payroll.

I also suspected people might be going through my office papers. In an attempt to confuse them and throw them off, I launched an attack of my own, leaving esoteric notes and curious messages. One said, "Operation Zebra underway. Three senators contacted, and all agree to come onboard. Secrecy absolute requirement. Tell no one." Another note said, "Dr. X of Stuttgart not sure he wants to talk on phone. Will meet with him at duck club to discuss new Senate rule."

Over time, I had numerous blowouts with Max Howell, and I kept notes about them. I think the senator respected me at times for standing up to him, but I know he resented the hell out of me for doing some of the things I did. One of the first major changes that Howell bucked was an audit of the Senate books, perhaps because he simply didn't believe it was necessary and also because he might have considered it an attempt to question his management skills, which had kept the Senate going for several decades.

Howell's one secretary, who answered only to him, had credit cards that only she could use. The old secretary was very cordial to me after I arrived on the scene, but it was very clear that she only answered to Max Howell. She was eventually "retired" from service after a payday fiasco.

When we cleaned out her desk, a fellow employee and I found huge stacks of old uncashed state payroll checks and W-2 forms bearing names of people I had never heard of. My longtime friend from Sheridan in the state auditor's office was in charge of all state payrolls, and I phoned him. He walked up to the office, and I showed him the stack of papers. He said he had no knowledge of the checks but that Senator Howell always paid him $500 extra from the state to handle all the Senate payroll. He said he considered it a small favor and "an honor" to handle the payroll for the ranking legislator and that he always processed the checks and always handed them over to Howell's secretary, who he assumed distributed them to the employees.

After finding the papers, I asked my assistant to destroy them and not say a word to anyone about what we had found. But I always wondered who those people were and if the checks might have been issued in error and just set aside by mistake. Perhaps the secretary simply forgot they were hidden under the mat on her desk or failed to put them in the mail.

Not only did I get an earful from Howell about my friendship with Mr. Witt Stephens, I also received a full-blown attack after he found out that I was a loyal supporter of Dale Bumpers. Bumpers was one of state's US senators when I accepted the Senate job in 1985, and he was seeking reelection to his post in Washington. I had always liked and supported Bumpers and had helped him in my native Grant County, serving as one of his campaign chairmen.

Soon after taking the Senate job, Kelley Erstine, a Sheridan friend, joined with me in hosting a Dale Bumpers fund-raiser at my house in Sheridan. The local paper ran a photo of Bumpers and me along with a short article about the event.

It wasn't long till Howell got wind of it, and he was promptly at my office door in the Senate. He wanted to know how serious I was about supporting Bumpers.

"I've always supported him from the very first time he ran for governor," I explained. "I was a very young reporter when he first ran, and I was assigned to cover him, and I got to know him."

This did not sit well with Howell, who then explained why he deplored the man.

"You know he refuses to come to my roast-and-toast every year in Sherwood," Howell began.

"No, sir, I was not aware of that," I answered.

"Well, he won't, and besides that, he's against the Star Wars [satellite defense] project in Congress, and someone in my family works on that," Howell raged.

Once again, I had to pull out all stops in massaging the man's ego in order to settle him down.

"Senator Howell, what's between you and Senator Bumpers, that's your business," I began. "But one reason you asked me to come to work for you was that I had a lot of political experience and I knew a lot of people, and maybe my being here can turn out to be a plus for you in this."

I was doing my best and reaching for the stars in trying to head him off.

"Well, maybe," he said, starting to calm down.

"Tell you what," I said. "Next time I see Dale or talk with him, I'll ask him if he might look at his schedule in the future and consider coming to your roast-and-toast."

Howell grinned and walked away. I never did tell Dale about the roast or about my conversation with Howell.

I mentioned William Parks, the young black man from Morrilton who came to work for me early on in the Senate. William was the reason Howell almost fired me less than two years after my initial employment.

A photographer is hired during each legislative session to take the official photos of the senators. A huge composite made up of all the senators and a few selected staff is then put together and hung outside the Senate chamber. This job was left to me to supervise, and after the senators picked out their favorite photo, I selected a few of the staff that I wanted depicted on the composite. All the new Senate staff were selected, including the young Parks, but once again, this infuriated Howell.

At first, Howell's loyal secretary who had worked at the Senate a very long time "suggested" that Parks not be placed in the large photo composite. "No," I explained to her, "William is a full-time employee, and I want him in there."

"Well," she huffed, "Senator Howell is not going to like that."

"And why is that?" I asked her pointedly, knowing the reason but trying to bait her into telling me.

"Well, he just won't."

I knew the reason, and it was because Parks was black, and there could be no other reason.

In less than an hour, after my conversation with the secretary, my phone rang, and it was the senior senator.

"I hear you're putting people you want in the composite," he said.

"I met with the photographer, yes, sir, I did," I answered, "but that's what you asked me to do."

"I don't recall asking you to put your favorite people on there," he said abruptly.

"Senator Howell, I don't want to go through a lot of this about a photo, all due respect."

"Well, my secretary and I don't think we need to be putting our janitor on the photo display," he argued.

"Sir, William is a part of our brand-new permanent staff, and he's a constituent of Senator Gordon, and I'd hate to be the one to tell William or Senator Gordon that we put all seven or our permanent staff on the composite and left off one. That just isn't right, is it?"

"Well, I'll make that call."

"Tell you what, Senator Howell. I'll make it easy for you."

"How's that?"

"Let's leave my photo off, and William can take my slot."

"I don't like the sound of that," he shot back.

"Well, if William isn't on there, Senator, and all due respect again, I don't think I want to be around to tell him why some people here did not want him on there."

"I'm hanging up now," he said. And he did.

The secretary informed me the next morning that Howell had decided that all the permanent staff should be pictured. I never told William about the episode, but it was another indication that I was up against some staggering odds in trying to do my job and trying to do it the right way.

CHAPTER 14

My indoctrination into the world of the Arkansas Senate got off to a fast start. Early on, I watched two senators die. They were John Bearden and Tom Watson, both of whom were personal favorites.

John Bearden was extremely intelligent and a member of the East Arkansas Bearden family that served the Senate for decades. One night, we were working late. His office was across the hall from mine, and he called out to me.

"I'm not feeling very well. I may need a little help in here."

I rushed to the office, and John was throwing up. "I think you might ought to get your governor to the hospital," he said jokingly.

The reason he said this was because Governor Clinton and Lieutenant Governor Winston Bryant were out of state, and Bearden was the acting governor. (When the governor and lieutenant governor are out of state, the Senate president pro tem ascends to the governorship.)

I literally picked him up and got him to an elevator, where security guards helped me get him into a car and into the hospital emergency room. The press started calling because his illness was newsworthy since he was acting governor. Not long after the hospital stay, John Bearden died.

I remember Senator Tom Watson's final days in the hospital because of what he whispered in my ear. His wife and son were in the room, and Tom, a very quiet, shy legislator, didn't want to speak loudly. He motioned for me to go to his side, and he gently tugged on my tie to pull me closer. "Listen to me," he began, "you be careful, you hear me? Some of those people out there will cut your throat and watch you bleed to death."

Needless to say, I was speechless. Little did I know so early in my career at the Arkansas Senate how right, how prophetic, the old man from Monette had been with that warning. He died the next day, and he had a well-attended funeral, but my thoughts that day revolved around another funeral and another run-in with senior senator Howell.

It started when Bill Darling, my dear friend, walked into my office at the Senate. Bill was the Senate information director and a member of my new staff. He had been a friend since we worked together in the 1970s at the *Pine Bluff Commercial* newspaper. He walked in to tell me that his doctor had confirmed he had cancer and that he had only a few months to live.

I was devastated and held Bill while he cried, trying as much as I could to hold back my own tears. He was at a loss about what to do in his last remaining days, how he would break the news to his wife and three small kids. I tried to advise him, knowing I would fall apart too, as soon as he left my office.

A few weeks passed, and the cancer moved quickly. Bill started taking sick days to try to cope. Bill had become close to Senator Ben Allen of Little Rock, and Ben was naturally concerned about the situation. The senator and I talked and agreed that perhaps the best thing we could do would be to raise money to help pay Bill's funeral expenses. We called on as many people as we knew, and the work made the two of us feel a little better.

In the meantime, I decided to ask Senator Howell, in his role as chairman of the Efficiency Committee, to consider raising Bill to his maximum salary level. This would mean a $10 a week raise. My goal was not the extra few dollars my friend might net over the remaining few months of his life, but how the extra benefit might impact survival benefits to Bill's wife and three children.

"I'll call an Efficiency meeting to discuss it," Howell growled back at me when I asked.

A meeting was called. Back then, the committee consisted of only five members. Shortly before the meeting was to convene at 10:00

a.m., I ran into Senator Nick Wilson in the Senate Quiet Room, a lavishly appointed private lounge.

"What's our meeting about?" Wilson asked me while reaching for a phone to make a call.

"I want to ask the committee to give Bill Darling a salary increase before he dies," I answered.

"How long does he have?" Wilson asked politely.

"About two months at the most."

"And we gotta have a meeting to vote on something like that?" Wilson asked.

"Senator Howell said we did," I answered.

Wilson became furious, and I was glad that he was seeing what I was going through at the time.

Soon, the meeting began, and all five members pulled up a chair. Senator Clarence Bell, my friend, started the conversation. "What's this about, Max?" he said, glaring at Howell.

Before Howell could say a word, Wilson interrupted. "I move [make a motion] that we move Bill Darling's salary to the maximum level."

"I second the motion," Allen shot back.

Howell was slam-dunked before he ever picked up the gavel. "Well, I can see the chairman's been railroaded in his own meeting," he snapped, looking in my direction. "If there's no other business, meeting's adjourned."

We walked from the room, and standing near the Senate elevator, I turned to Howell and said, "Thank you, Senator Howell."

"Hey, Bill," he began with a statement that sent my blood pressure into orbit. "You don't have to thank me. I was in the military, you know. I know where you're comin' from. You get the pay of your subordinates up, and then you know we have to raise your pay, right?"

Every emotion I'd ever experienced surged through my body. I thought I would explode. This man whom I was trying to respect was standing toe-to-toe next to me, and all I could think of was that he was insulting me and my character at a time when my friend is dying, forcing his colleagues to call a meeting just to vote on giving a dead man's widow a pension, and he hurled this kind of heartless insult at me.

"I tell you what, Senator Howell, whatever the hell I got coming to me, ever, you give it to the man's wife and kids!" I said in a huffed tone as I stormed away to my nearby office.

I was told later that he was left standing alone as his colleagues turned their backs on him. Like me, they felt totally disgusted.

I sat in my office, crying like a child. My emotion for my friend had finally poured out, and I couldn't shut it off. Then a light tap on the door. It was Senator Howell. He asked to go in.

"Hey, I was out of line," he said.

"Senator Howell, I cannot believe you would say that."

"I'm sorry."

That episode passed, and we continued to lock horns occasionally. I saw with each passing day that he sorely resented the new staff, then the strange episode with the new phones, and then, to pour more salt into my wounds, he ordered that the staff keep daily work reports, writing down every single thing we do.

Beebe and the younger senators were appalled at this suggestion, knowing that it was Howell's way of keeping tabs on just who among the membership were calling on staff for help. Howell had all the help he needed at his downtown law firm and three or four stooges on the Legislative Council staff, but he wanted more; he wanted to know what the Senate staff was doing for the membership.

Adept at playing childish games, I complied with the request to keep up with daily chores so that Howell would receive my report each Friday. Day after day, week after week, I and the others would write down every single thing we did. It became a game as I computerized and recorded all the activities. I kept all the data in a big notebook. On some days, there were dozens of requests and projects. A sample is this report from Monday, 23 October 1989:

- Took call from B. Allen, constituent against tax, took message.
- Talked with Sen. Moore, re: booklets.
- Asked staff attorney to do Steve Bell project.
- Got speech assignment from M. Beebe.
- Made pot of coffee.
- Clipped newspapers.
- Met w/staff re: computer program.

- Discussed with staff about help for Gibson, Gordon, Scott radio programs.
- Took instructions by phone from Jon Fitch.
- Delivered Fitch message to Sen. Beebe.
- Met with governor's assistant needing instructions on delivery.
- Introduced the assistant to Hal Moody.
- Met with Sen. Gibson re: session faxes and newspapers.
- Met with Lloyd George re: where drug meeting to be held.
- Sent BB tape to Kay Goss.
- Met with Yates, Gibson re: lunch request.
- Worked up "volunteerism" speech for Sen. Walters.
- Asked staff attorney to fax materials to Sen. Walters.
- Worked on resolution at Sen. Fitch's request.
- Presented resolution to Sen. Beebe.
- Wrote radio program.
- Distributed radio program.
- Met with Sen. S. Bell re: session length report.
- Wrote SR for Knox and Jay.
- Bio of books to Alexander.

This was a sample of a day's work at the Senate, where I had thirty-five political bosses. And all staff were having to do the reports and file them at the close of business each week with me. I would then forward them to Howell.

This went on for two years until Howell phoned one day. "I can't believe the report you turned in Friday," he began. "You can't put that on paper!"

"You ordered me to put down everything I do, and that's what I did, Senator," I answered.

"What if the press gets hold of this?" he asked.

"Well, sir, I guess they have that right. But to answer your question, I suppose it would be embarrassing."

"Well, I'll be out there in a minute, and we'll talk about this some more."

He arrived in a matter of minutes. What had him upset was my listing of a "project" I carried out at the Capitol Hill apartment building. One of the senators who had an apartment there phoned me in a panic. He asked me to hustle over to the apartment, remove any "suspicious" ladies' garments that I found, and strip the sheets off the bed and get them laundered before his wife got to town—which I did. I also put all this in my report, which infuriated Howell.

"You asked me to write down everything I did each day, and there it is," I said to him in my office.

"Then that's the end of these reports. No more."

With that, he walked out, and the reports ended. My plan had worked to perfection. Ask and ye shall receive, I had learned early in life in my Sunday school classes at the Christian church. Or as Barney told Andy, "With shortsighted directives, you end up with inexperienced policemen."

Another time we stood toe-to-toe, I and ol' Max, this time over his attempt to have "storm" windows installed in the Senate offices. It just so happened that Howell had a "friend" in the window business, and the esteemed chairman had decided our offices needed the fix-up. Of course, no bids were taken, and this friend of Howell's showed up to begin the work. I questioned him and asked him to wait outside my office until I got confirmation about what he was to do. This sent Howell into orbit. He ordered me over the phone to let the man begin the work, which I did. To my amazement, the storm windows consisted of a large sheet of razor-thin plastic that was stuck to the window facing and sealed with a hair dryer. When I asked about the cost, the worker said he would send the bill to Senator Howell.

A few weeks later, in an Efficiency Committee meeting, Howell mentioned to his colleagues that he had ordered this questionable work done. Questions were raised about it, and Howell began to suspect that I had said something derogatory about the man's work, which I had not. After the meeting, he confronted me face-to-face. "You said something to Clarence," Howell said, referring to vice chairman, Bell.

"No, sir, I did not," I answered.

At that moment, Bell, a big man, rose slowly and turned on Howell. "Nobody said a word to me—I just think that project's for the birds."

Howell then looked at me and said, "I'll do what I want out here. You ain't got a say in any of it."

I lost my cool and said, "Senator Howell, I don't give a fiddly fuck about that project."

Late that day, I traveled to Jonesboro for Arkansas State University football weekend. My staffer, William Parks, and I set up a hospitality suite at the Holiday Inn, and I had refreshments for visiting legislators and guests who attended the ball game and festivities. My room became a popular stopover before and after the game.

The first person to go by that afternoon was Senator Clarence Bell. William poured him a bourbon and water, and Clarence began to chuckle. "Bill," he said to me, "what was that word you said to ol' Max today when y'all were arguing? I was trying to think of it on the way up here to tell my wife."

"I don't know, Senator Bell. I shouldn't have said that to Senator Howell."

"Naw, I get a kick out of all that, but it was a word I've never heard before. It tickled me."

"*Fiddly fuck*—I said *fiddly fuck*."

"Yeah, that was it. What does that mean?"

"It just means, I don't give a flip. I was telling Max I didn't give a flip about the windows."

"Boy, that was something."

Clarence liked the way I stood my ground with Howell. And boy, did I like Clarence Bell. His funeral was a lot different from Howell's. I was honored to be a pallbearer for C. Bell—me, Skip Rutherford, and some other great guys. Clarence Bell deserved a special place in heaven as far as I was concerned. He was a true prince.

Two other stories come to mind that demonstrated what some saw as Howell's arrogance and quick temper.

Joe Yates was an easygoing Republican senator from Northwest Arkansas (more about him later). On this day, Yates and his wife, Anita, had journeyed down to the capitol cafeteria for a quick lunch, and a line had formed a few feet away from the buffet service. Howell and two other senators walked up and got in the line behind Yates and his wife. Yates turned to talk to Howell, and Anita turned with him and started to say something to her husband. "Hey, don't you interrupt two senators when they're talking." Howell opened up on the unsuspecting woman. "Nobody comes between me and one of my fellow senators."

Yates, remaining calm as he always did, interrupted the angry Howell and said, "Hey, Max, maybe I ought to introduce you, this is my old lady, Anita, my wife."

Howell fell all over himself trying to apologize. Understandably, Mrs. Yates never had very many nice things to say about the ranking member of the upper chamber after that experience.

The same kind of thing happened one day outside the huge House chamber. A committee made up of senators and House members had been assigned to walk down to the second floor and escort new governor Frank White up to the third floor to address the joint session of the legislature. This is common procedure at the start of a legislative session.

The senators and House members were making their way to the top of the giant marble staircase with the new, excited chief executive in tow. Howell was waiting for the delegation at the top of the stairs, and as they arrived at the House door, he pushed Representative Lacy Landers of Benton aside, almost making him stumble, and instructed Landers, "Nobody comes between me and my governor."

Later that afternoon, Landers was still fuming and asked me, "Did you see what Max Howell did out there to me?"

I told him I was as shocked as the rest of the crowd, who witnessed it. "The saddest part is," I told Landers, "Senator Howell was probably so carried away with things he didn't ever know who you were."

"You're right about that," Landers said. "Max being Max."

CHAPTER 15

S peaking of Arkansas State University and its football weekends, I probably saved that school from Max Howell's eternal wrath. No, let me rephrase that—I most definitely saved that school from Max Howell's eternal wrath. My friend, lobbyist Don Tilton, was employed at ASU and had not gone into lobbying work when this happened. It was 1989, and ASU was set to honor Senator Howell during pregame festivities for his longtime legislative support. Years earlier, Max and I were discussing deer hunting in my office, and he mentioned that he had killed a giant elk one time in Colorado. He said he kept the elk head for years, a prized mount, but that it had ended up at Arkansas State, where he presented the animal to one of the presidents to be displayed in a new building.

As Tilton and the ASU brass prepared for Senator Howell's weekend visit, Tilton phoned to go over program details. I remembered the elk story and mentioned to Don that Max might want to visit the building to see his old trophy.

There was this long silence on the phone. "We ain't got no elk up here, Scoop," Don said to me, calling me by my nickname. "I don't know what you're talking about."

I explained the story again, saying that Howell had given his prized kill to the university as a valued gift. Tilton said he would go to work immediately.

A few days later, Howell and his wife, Inez, pulled up to my room at the Holiday Inn. I was expecting them, and Senator Howell greeted me and asked me if I would mind driving them to the university campus for the president's dinner. I told him I would be happy to drive and that I would enjoy being in his new white Chrysler, which he had told me about.

The three of us arrived, and Tilton was standing at the entrance. He smiled at me and introduced the Howells to various dignitaries. Not missing a beat, the senior senator asked Tilton, "Where's the building with my elk?"

Not missing a beat either, Tilton said, "Yes, sir. I'm glad you remembered your elk, Senator. Come with us." Tilton and the Howells walked away into a nearby building where Tilton proudly displayed the elk that had been donated fifteen years earlier. That night, in private, Tilton told me what he had done.

"We found the elk in storage, in a basement. I worked all day getting it ready, cleaning it up, and getting it hung on the wall. God, Scoop, you saved this university. You really did."

It was a fun weekend.

CHAPTER 16

My job as chief of staff was a fly-by-the-seat-of-my-pants operation because no one had preceded me in the position. So I had to use my knowledge, instincts, and newspapering skills to blaze this new territory.

Besides catering to thirty-five prima donnas, which mostly was a pleasant task, I also had to pay special attention to the president pro tem. This is the person who, by constitutional authority, is second in line of succession to the governor. He is, for two years, also the figurehead of the Senate, although seniority usually rules the roost.

But I got to work with some very talented pro tems. Not all were stellar, mind you, but some were. Mike Beebe was a favorite because he was a favorite overall and the man who led me to the upper chamber in 1985. He delegated much of the pro tem work and ceremonial duties to colleagues, which was his style of governing, a style that carried over into his successful tenure as governor.

It will surprise some people reading this when I say Nick Wilson was also a favorite pro tem of mine. Nick was a rascal and on the other side of the fence from Beebe in most things, but he made his time as pro tem an enjoyable period simply because he wanted the very best for the Senate. He wanted things first-class, and so did I.

I remember one issue in particular. The chiropractors association had placed a vibrating chiropractor couch in the private members' lounge in the House. The House members could go into the room and lie down on the couch, and the rotating tumblers would stretch their back muscles. It was a hot topic of conversation as one of the legislative sessions got underway.

The chiropractors approached the Senate about putting one of the couches in the Senate Quiet Room, where senators could enjoy some of the same pleasures afforded their colleagues in the House. The Senate Quiet Room was a beautiful, historic room, artfully appointed with rich leather furniture and mahogany tables.

Senator Howell called a meeting of the Efficiency Committee to discuss whether or not to allow one of the special couches to be placed in the room. Nick asked me before the meeting what I thought about the idea, and I said I thought it might be a conflict of interest since the chiropractors were lobbying for some special legislation. I thought the couches could lead to bad publicity for the senators, and besides that, I thought a vibrating couch was actually beneath what the Senate and its historic room stood for. As I talked, he grinned and chomped on his cigar.

That afternoon, the Efficiency Committee settled in, and Max Howell immediately got to the agenda, which meant a discussion of the couch. Wilson wasted little time and, just to get the pot to boil, turned to me and asked me for my thoughts on the subject.

"Well, if you really want to know what I think, I think it's a horrible idea," I said.

This, of course, infuriated Howell, who said, "Well, let's hear what the members have to say."

Bell, apparently alerted by Wilson, said, "I vote no. We don't have room in here for that thing. If any of the senators want a rubdown, they can walk down to the House and stand in line."

Howell then turned to me. "So you're against this?" he asked politely.

"Senator Howell, please don't put a vibrating couch in this room," I began. "Look at this room. It's the most beautiful room in the capitol, and a lot of that credit goes to you. You've been here longer than anyone, your plaque with your picture is in here, and people want to put your picture next to a vibrating couch?"

I gave it my all. Nick sat back and kept grinning. As a compromise, I spoke up again and suggested if some of the senators wanted a couch, perhaps we could find room for it in what we called the Senate pharmacy, a small room near the third floor refreshment stand, where medical assistance was available during legislative sessions. My suggestion pleased Howell, and on Howell's motion, the committee voted to accept the chiropractors' offer but to see to it the couch was located down the hall and away from the Senate's well-appointed lounge called the Quiet Room.

Near the end of my career, the Senate, long after Howell had departed, spent several million dollars in a complete renovation of the huge chamber, all the offices, and the Quiet Room. In the back of the room, renovators uncovered some old plaster where the architect of the capitol building had written his name more than a hundred years earlier. I asked them to place a see-through window box around the signature so that it could be saved. People marveled at this historic relic. It was located on the south wall of the room, right above where the vibrating couch might have been placed had Nick and the others not intervened.

One other favorite Max Howell story and it demonstrated again how, like Charlie Cole Chaffin suggested, you have to stand your ground against certain things—I, along with several senators, journeyed to Reno, Nevada, for a national legislative meeting, or, as the press would always say, another junket. And to be honest, a lot of the trips were just that—vacation junkets at taxpayers' expense.

We had spent two days in Reno when Mike Beebe and Jon Fitch suggested we take a side trip to Lake Tahoe, a two-hour drive from our hotel. Several of the senators and their wives wanted to tour the famous vacation spot, and Beebe suggested I check into renting two or three vans for the trip.

A van rental business was a short walk from my hotel, and I rented three vans and put the cost on my personal credit card. After returning home and going back to work at the Senate, I turned in my expenses for the trip. This meant I turned in my forms to Howell's secretary, the woman who had worked at the Senate for years and checked with Howell on everything.

It took only a few minutes for my phone to ring. It was the ranking senator, of course, calling from his downtown law office.

"What's this charge for van rentals out there on that trip?" he began in a sharp, angry tone.

"Three vans, Senator Howell," I answered. "Several of the senators and their wives wanted to make a day trip to Lake Tahoe, and I rented some vans for the trip and put the cost on my credit card."

"I ain't payin' for no fancy trip to some lake," he growled.

"That's fine," I answered. "I didn't know what to do, really, when the senators asked me to get the vans. I'll be happy to call Senator Beebe and tell him you don't want to pay for his van."

"Now, wait a damn minute," he shot back. "I, well, I didn't mean it that way. Uh, well, we'll cover it this time, but you ain't gonna broker these deals."

"Senator Howell, all due respect, I didn't broker any kind of deal. I rented three vans because the senators asked me to get them three vans. That's the whole thing."

"Fine," he said, about to hang up. "Don't call anybody."

My reimbursement check was placed on my desk the next day by the smiling secretary.

Our love for golf took us on so many journeys and to some beautiful places. One of the most memorable trips was to Florida, where several of us were the guests of Alltel telephone company. The company, founded in Arkansas, was expanding a new customer service program, and they wanted Beebe and his group to see the company's facility near Jacksonville. After work, we decided to spend some extra time and play golf, but we weren't sure even then where our journey would end.

Senator Bill Gwatney said it would be an added treat if we were able to play a round of golf on the famous Sawgrass course at Ponte Vedra Beach, a ninety-minute drive from our hotel. A telephone call was made, but we were told the course would be closed the following day for the club's annual membership tournament.

But the Young Golfers were known for their tenacity, so deciding not to give up just yet, another phone call was made, this time to former Arkansas state senator Joe Ford in Little Rock. Ford, the president of the Alltel company, was also a well-known member of Augusta Country Club in Georgia and a close friend of Dean Beaman, the big cheese commissioner of the Professional Golfers Association. Our goal was to persuade Ford to give Beaman a courtesy call and ask if he could possibly work out something with the Sawgrass club. It was a shot in the dark, but we knew it was a chance worth taking. In less than an hour, Ford called back to say he had talked with his good friend and that a plan had come together. We were told to be at the Sawgrass pro shop at 7:30 a.m. the following day, no later, and that our group could play the famous course. We had to be off the course by noon so that the members' tournament could begin. The miracle plan had come together because of our Arkansas connections and the good-old-boy political network that was proving once again to be beneficial.

Early the next day, we teed off on the famous course with the ominous island green. We finished up in plenty of time and were safely aboard our private jet en route back home to Arkansas by midday, another wonderful memory to treasure for a very long time.

CHAPTER 17

The Arkansas Senate Quiet Room—I honestly think that place caused me more grief than any other part of my job had. I say that because the room was off-limits to everyone except the senators, House members, myself, and the secretary of the Senate. Senator Howell and his successors put me in charge of enforcing the rule.

During legislative sessions, I posted security sergeants at both entrances of the room to keep unauthorized persons out. When the legislature was not in session, this task was left up to me, and it was not an easy task to enforce.

In fact, this rule cost me more friends than anything and hurt my standing with several members.

Sharon Trusty was a very capable senator from Russellville and someone I liked a great deal. But her husband, Fritz, would sneak into the room to retrieve a soft drink or Popsicle. I "caught" him once and asked him not to go into the room, and a senator went to the office to complain about him returning to the room. I asked Sharon to please alert her husband to the problem, and I think it made her upset with me, which I regretted.

Other frequent abusers were Senator Kevin Smith's small children. More than once, I found them sneaking into the room to get Popsicles, and I repeatedly asked the lovable Smith to please corral his youngsters.

In fact, we started the legislative session one afternoon, and Smith was nowhere to be found. Beebe and others asked me to see if I could find him. My search was futile, but after about an hour, Smith showed up in my office.

"Where have you been?" I asked excitedly.

"I have some news, and I wanted you to be the first person here to know it," he began. "We've been to the doctor, me and my wife, and she's going to have twins . . . she's pregnant."

"Oh god," I replied. "We'll never be able to keep Popsicles in the Quiet Room now."

To show another softer side of Nick Wilson, another Quiet Room memory comes to mind. It was during the time Wilson was serving as pro tem, and his workload, which was already heavy, had picked up even more dramatically. I was returning to my third-floor office late in the day when I looked into the Quiet Room and saw Wilson sitting with his top assistant and other members of his office staff. They were going through huge stacks of paper, and from all appearances, it looked as if they were facing a long night of work.

I went on into my office, but the following morning, I asked Wilson for a moment.

"This isn't easy for me to talk about, but I need to ask your help with something," I began.

"Sure, what is it?" he asked.

"Yesterday, you were working in the Quiet Room with Cathy and the others, and well, you know I've been asked to keep everyone out of there unless those who are authorized, and it puts me in a very sensitive place."

"Never even entered my mind," he said. "You're right. I shouldn't have had them back there, and next time, we'll work here in my office. Don't sweat it. You got a job to do."

End of the conversation, but I worried that I had made another boss uneasy with me.

The best-kept secret about the Senate Quiet Room involved my clandestine work with the Arkansas State Police. Only Mike Beebe and I knew the details of this episode, which involved undercover surveillance of the big room and its adjoining kitchen.

My properties officer, William Parks, told me he had noticed that someone had been sneaking into the kitchen area after closing time, perhaps in the wee hours past midnight, and taking beverages and cold snacks such as the popular and tasty Fudgsicles—one of my favorites.

It wasn't an earthshaking felonious development, but I became more concerned after we noticed that one of the large brass locks on the door leading from the Quiet Room into the kitchen had been damaged, apparently by the intruder, who looked to be using a screwdriver to scratch on the door.

I informed Beebe, the pro tem at the time, and I told him I thought it was serious enough to alert authorities. He asked if this meant the capitol police, which had a force of about ten officers, but I said a better option might be the state police since I suspected some of the capitol police might be the very ones doing the breaking and eating.

We laughed a little bit about it, but it was becoming a serious situation since the senators' offices were located adjacent to the area being vandalized.

I met with two state police specialists who devised a plan. It would amount to me placing a radio, much like the ones used in a person's home, near the kitchen refrigerator. But this was no ordinary radio; it was a special camera, which was motion-activated. I would activate the switch when I left in the afternoon, and if someone entered the room, it would record their activity on a video tape, which I could review the next day.

I baited the trap and anxiously watched for almost a week, advising Beebe that no one had shown up on the tape. But on day 5, we hit pay dirt. I couldn't believe my eyes as I watched the night clean-up man for the secretary of state's office creeping slowly into the room. He methodically removed cans of Coke and other tasty treats from the refrigerator, placed them in his large trash-hauling cart, and slowly closed the door behind him.

I alerted Beebe the next day that we had our man, but the bad news was that it was the well-known and mentally challenged cleanup man who worked for the secretary of state.

I met with the man's supervisors and the captain of the capitol police and told them what had happened. We didn't want to pursue the matter, and I left it up to the man's bosses to handle the situation. The funny part of the story was that the only other person we caught on the tape was Senator Jay Bradford, walking into the room late at night, to mix up a drink. We never told Jay he was caught on film, not that he would have cared. We all liked having a refreshment at the end of our workday, and the kitchen was a nice place to take care of that little chore.

After Senator Jack Gibson left the Senate, he lobbied for a short time. The new legislative session was about to get underway when Gibson showed up at the Senate. He had spent several years there as a senator, and it was second nature for him to walk around and greet the people. In doing this, he absentmindedly walked into the Quiet Room, a place where he had spent countless hours as a senator. He chatted with several people and then left, making his way past my office.

I asked my old friend to come in for a chat. We exchanged pleasantries, and then I got to my real point of the conversation. "Jack," I began, carefully selecting my words, "you can't go back there to the Quiet Room again. You're a lobbyist now and not a member, okay?"

"Damn, Scoop, you kickin' me out?" He laughed.

"Yep, I'm kickin' you out of the Quiet Room. If you need coffee or a snack, you can hang out here in my office, okay?"

"I love you, man," he said, standing to shake my hand. "Hang in there."

Besides the Quiet Room, another pain in the rear for me and Massanelli over in the House were the legislative license plates.

Each senator and House member is given a couple of special license plates to put on their cars. It's a big ego trip, to have a special license plate that shows the world that you are a duly elected legislator. Police officers usually defer to the tags and give legislators a break on their speeding, and the plates can guarantee special parking privileges at a number of places.

But they also can show up in places that can lead to controversy and embarrassment. That's when I got the telephone calls, and it took a lot of diplomatic wrangling to undo the damage and potential public relations damage.

Usually, the calls were about speeding, angry motorists calling me to report they had seen a senator pass them at breakneck speeds. And there were calls about cars being seen in suspicious places, sometimes late at night, and these calls were extremely sensitive.

One such call came in as I arrived early in the morning. A woman said a man driving a Senate-tagged car had parked outside her office the night before and that the senator was "carrying on" with a blond-headed woman. She went into great detail, more than I actually wanted to hear. I assured her I would check into the matter, and I launched into my usual spin about how we had gotten reports on similar sightings and that the Senate tags were being confused with some newly issued tags being distributed by another department of state government. It was total BS on my part, but I was doing my spin magic, trying to settle the caller down and confuse her at the same time.

Later that day, I confronted the senator who had been implicated, and we had a good heart-to-heart talk about the benefits and dangers of legislative license plates and staying out late at the bars. He smiled sheepishly and thanked me, and not another word was ever spoken about the incident.

A similar situation occurred in the House when a former House member refused to do away with his tags. When a legislator leaves office, he is required to remove the tags from his car, but an ex-legislator from Morrilton refused to comply with this policy. Consequently, the new House member who received the ex-member's tag number was implicated in a controversy in North Little Rock—turns out that the former member was driving his car with the outdated tag when he was arrested in North Little Rock. The following day, the North Little Rock newspaper reported the arrest and said it appeared the car belonged to the new state representative from North Little Rock. The new representative was wrongly implicated because of the bogus tag, and soon the real story came out. The House leadership finally sent the state police to the ex-member's home, and the officers removed the special tag and destroyed it.

The only benefit to the tags was they allowed the capitol police and my office to monitor parking at the capitol. Each senator was assigned a specific parking space, which corresponded with the license plates. This way, we could monitor the parking and ensure security, which was a high priority at the capitol at times, especially after the terrorist attacks on 9-11. But bottom line, legislative license plates were a pain and not worth the trouble they caused.

Speaking of pro tems and Nick Wilson, I won't forget Stanley Russ's tenure as pro tem. Russ had a pristine reputation among the news media, but Wilson and others, including Jon Fitch, didn't care much for the Conway lawmaker. When it became time for Russ's end-of-session pro tem party, he suggested I start putting the plans together as I had done for other pro tems but to make sure everyone understood there would be no booze served at the dinner.

Later, Russ let me know he had selected a church as the dinner location, and everyone had been alerted that if they wanted an alcohol cocktail, they had best tune up before arriving at the church because it was a teetotaling affair.

We were all seated and ready for supper when I glanced up; atop the big church staircase and walking down the stairs were Nick Wilson, Allen Gordon, and Mike Bearden. We knew they would be late because they had taken the cocktail warning seriously and had stayed a little longer at their favorite watering hole. I was wishing I had been with them because dealing with this type of social outing was an ultimate nightmare.

Russ had upset me earlier in the week, and it was another time I had to stand my ground with a boss. Senator Kevin Smith of Stuttgart was having a rough time with one of the governor's staff members, and according to an angry Smith, the two of them had almost come to blows in a committee meeting downstairs from the Senate offices. Smith was telling me about this when I pulled a Senate attorney aside and asked him to hear Smith's story along with me. I was trying to console the young senator, whom we had affectionately nicknamed Young Pup, when Russ walked up.

Russ butted in and asked my assistant to go with him immediately to address a problem. "I'll be right with you, Senator Russ," the assistant said to the Conway lawmaker.

This angered Russ, who shot back, "Oh well, maybe I need to reintroduce myself to you all. I'm Stanley Russ, and I'm the pro tem, and I've been here a lot longer than Senator Smith!"

I was floored by the comment and Russ's abrupt behavior. I had never seen that side of him, and I knew I had to respond. I told my assistant to stay with Smith, and I asked Russ to step into his office, which was a few feet away.

"Now, listen—" he began with me, only to be interrupted.

"Senator Russ," I said in one of my sharper tones, "what in the world is going on? That's not like you to act like that, and you need to be nicer to that young senator out there because I think he thinks the world of you."

I was doing my best to handle the man with every conciliatory approach I could muster.

He took a deep breath and leaned back against the long worktable in the small office.

"I made a fool of myself out there, didn't I?" he offered.

"Well, you sure did," I answered.

He said he would go out and correct the situation immediately, and from what I was told, he did just that.

The most fractious pro tem was Jerry Bookout of Jonesboro. He was nearing the end of a long career, and he found himself adrift in the ongoing turf war with Howell, Nelson, Beebe, and Wilson. Bookout postured as one of Beebe's minions, and he did vote with Beebe's bunch in battles against Wilson; but privately, he seethed against Beebe, and his jealousy was obvious.

He despised Beebe for getting so much credit in taking care of Arkansas State University in Bookout's hometown. But the ASU folks knew that Beebe, an ASU grad and former ASU board chairman, was the new legislative leader, and they turned to him rather than Bookout almost daily when they needed financial help.

And Beebe didn't fully trust Bookout, knowing that his jealousy often led to rage. Bookout hated Nick Wilson and was constantly harping about Wilson behind the scenes. It became Bookout's number 1 mission to make Wilson's life miserable if he could, but he was no match for Wilson's ingenuity or knowledge of the system. If it came to a showdown between Wilson and Bookout, the big money would always ratchet down on Wilson.

I did everything I could to make Bookout's two-year tenure as pro tem as comfortable as possible, carefully walking the line between him and Wilson and Beebe. I bragged on his expensive suits and ties and laughed at his jokes, but deep down, I knew he didn't fully trust me because of my close allegiance to Beebe.

When the legislature traveled to Miami for the Southern Legislative Conference, I went two days early along with Massanelli and others in order to help SLC staff prepare for Bill Clinton, the presidential candidate who was scheduled to address the convention. Massanelli and I were to meet with Secret Service agents to prepare a list of Arkansas legislators who would lead Clinton into the auditorium for the big speech.

I asked Bookout if he would consider going early with us, and he liked the idea. He asked his wife to join us, and we arranged our flights to Florida. In my job, I frequently arranged for limo rides for the pro tem at official functions. I did so for Bookout and his wife, and when we arrived at the Miami airport, a stretch limo was waiting, and he was genuinely surprised when he noticed the chauffeur holding up a sign bearing his name. I looked at him and simply said, "Surprise."

I joined them in the limo ride to the world-famous Fontainebleau. As the limo squeezed into the circle drive, I could see dozens of people standing outside near the hotel's front entrance. They were staring at our car and waving frantically, and we craned our necks for a better view.

"Why in the world are they waving at us?" Bookout asked me in an excited tone.

"I ain't got a clue," I answered.

"Who do they think we are?" Loretta Bookout asked as the car pulled to a halt.

"Y'all stay inside the car, I'll handle this," I said, confidently reaching for the door handle.

I opened the door and stepped onto the curb, gesturing for the cheering crowd to step back.

"Y'all get back!" I shouted as I began pushing my open palms toward what appeared to be two dozen or so curious Japanese tourists. "I've got Jerry Bookout in here."

They peeled back toward the landscaped flowerbeds, and one by one they began mumbling, "Awe, Jerry Bookout. Jerry Bookout." Their mumbling became a low-pitched chant. "Jerry Bookout, Jerry Bookout, Jerry Bookout."

I reached back for the door, and Jerry and Loretta emerged from the shiny black limo. I thought he would bolt for the front entrance, but true to form, he began waving and smiling as though he had arrived right on cue, just as the crowd had expected. He waved more, and the thrilled spectators snapped photo after photo as we stepped briskly toward the front entrance, the crowd in tow.

We laughed until we couldn't laugh anymore. I told Bookout the Japanese tourists would return home with their cameras and that a whole generation of Japanese kids would grow up with Jerry Bookout's picture in their home, and they wouldn't know who in the hell he was. He loved the story, and it was told again at his funeral years later in Jonesboro. The man who told the story was Mike Beebe, the state's new governor, who delivered the eulogy.

I don't know why I stepped into the cheering crowd in Miami, but I did a lot of crazy things in my job. I remember flying to Fayetteville one evening with five senators for a Razorback basketball game. It was the last game at the old Barnhill Fieldhouse, and I wanted to be there when the Hogs played LSU. I had become a huge Nolan Richardson fan, and I was following the Hog basketballers everywhere when they were on their winning roll, so I talked several of my bosses into renting a plane and flying up from Little Rock to the game.

We rented a car at the airport and headed for the Fieldhouse. We were running a little late, and parking spaces were scarce. Senator David Malone of Fayetteville, a U of A professor, was one of the senators in the car. He kept telling me we wouldn't be able to find a parking place, but I was confident I could think of something.

We steered through the parking lots and headed toward the front entrance of the building, where we could see security policemen everywhere. A big officer stepped out into the middle of the pavement and waved me to a halt near a sea of orange security cones, which were strategically placed in the road to block off the entrance.

"Can I help you, sir?" the roly-poly policeman asked as he looked inside my window.

"Look, I don't have time to explain, but if I don't get these Arkansas senators into that building before the tip-off, it's my job, do you understand?" I shouted.

"Yes, sir, leave it to me," the man in the blue uniform offered back. "You go, sir."

With the speed of one of Nolan's pressing guards, the policeman hopped forward and started pushing the orange cones aside as he waved us through. One by one, we passed the officers until we were waved into the vacant parking space immediately in front of Barnhill Arena.

"You're gonna get me fired, Scoop," Senator Malone yelled at me as I hurried him inside.

"Don't worry about it!" I yelled back. "I do crap like this all the time."

Another time was at Nashville's famous Opryland Hotel, one of the largest hotels in the world. This massive edifice was about to host the Southern Legislative Conference, and we all thought this huge hotel would be accustomed to big crowds. But when I arrived at the long circle drive leading up to the front entrance, I could see a huge traffic jam. I had scheduled a 6:00 p.m. dinner for all the Arkansas senators who were already in their rooms and expecting me to arrive and give them details about the evening meal. I had planned to check in by 4:00 p.m. and have messages delivered to the senators' rooms by 4:30 p.m., detailing plans for the evening.

However, the traffic was backed up for a mile, and the cars were not moving. The clock was ticking, and I had sat in one spot for almost an hour. I knew I had to do something or face the wrath of my bosses, who were used to me making their social arrangements.

Desperate as the clock ticked near 4:00 p.m., I abandoned my car and started walking toward the front entrance about a hundred yards away. The bell captain, nattily attired in a lime green uniform complete with gold whistle and cap, began waving at me. "Sir, get back in your car!" he yelled at me. "Sir, you cannot leave your car, sir!"

"You, you come with me," I said confidently, taking him by his white-gloved hand. "You want to do what's best for the state of Tennessee, you'll come with me right now."

It was amazing what you could get away with if you just had the nerve and, well, crazy moxie.

"Yes, sir, what is the problem?" he asked as we stopped at the front door.

"The problem is if I don't get to the front desk and get these envelopes in some senators' mailboxes in time for a meeting tonight, the governor of Tennessee is going to, well, it's my job, and my wife and kids can't afford for me to lose my job, okay?"

"The governor? You said the governor?" he asked.

"Let's go, man, now!" I insisted.

The man blew on the whistle, and we hustled inside where I handed the envelopes to the concierge, who delivered them to the front desk. The dinner invitations were in the senators' rooms by four thirty; we had a wonderful dinner hosted by the Arkansas lobbyists, and I had an Absolut vodka cocktail as I told a few of my buddies about my check-in experience.

Oh, and the bell captain even went back and parked my car for me. I never saw him again during my four-day stay. But I don't think I saw the same two people twice the entire time. It was the biggest, gaudiest hotel I'd ever seen. Morril Harriman, a senator at the time, hated it so much he moved to another hotel. And I couldn't say I blamed him.

One other note on the trip to Miami. As we settled in there and prepared for Clinton's visit, we paused our first evening to enjoy a first-class dinner at the famed Fontainebleau. My secretary and I were the guests of John Greer, the premier lobbyist from Blue Cross and Blue Shield who had made the trip down from Little Rock. Greer was one of my favorite people, and I traveled often with him, and the two of us frequently teamed up in golf tournaments. We liked each other from the first time we met.

At dinner that evening, I took a bathroom break, and it turned out to be a very providential meeting for the soon-to-be president from Arkansas. I had made the journey to Miami and had, like other Arkansans, placed a lapel pin on my jacket with the message "Ask Me about My Governor." These lapel pins were collector items for Arkansas Democrats who were excited about our governor running for president.

As I prepared to leave the bathroom at the Fontainebleu, a man stopped me and asked about the lapel pin. "Oh, are you here in advance of Governor Bill Clinton?" the man asked.

"Well, yes," I answered. "I'm a part of the legislative meeting which is coming here," I added.

"So are you with Bill Clinton?" he pursued.

"No, not really. I'm from Arkansas, and I work with the legislature there."

"Oh, well, I want to know if you could possibly arrange for me and a few in my group to meet Bill Clinton," he asked.

The conversation continued for a few minutes, and as things turned out, the man explained that his Jewish group wished to meet with Clinton over the possibility of Clinton being a part of a hospital dedication in Greater Miami. I explained that I could not guarantee a meeting with the presidential candidate but that I would do what I could. I asked the man to meet me the next day, and I would see about getting him a moment with Clinton after he spoke to the legislative convention.

I was able to work out the meeting, and the man and a dozen or so of his friends met briefly with Clinton. After photos, they all departed, and I thought I had done my little part in arranging a meeting that could lead to Clinton rounding up a few more votes in Miami, especially in the Jewish community. Little did I know how much the little meeting would benefit our governor, however. In a few weeks, I started receiving checks in the mail from Miami made out to the Clinton campaign. The checks continued arriving for a few more days, and I phoned Betsey Wright to make the proper arrangements for them to be delivered to the Clinton presidential headquarters. My trip to the bathroom that evening had convinced me again that Clinton was one lucky dude, and nothing could possibly stand in his way of becoming our next president. I always wondered how much my bathroom stop and the little lapel button raised him in campaign contributions.

My association with John Greer was very special, and he became a lifelong friend. He took over the lobbying effort for Blue Cross after the big insurance company made a major lobbying mistake. The company was pressing hard on an issue, and in a last-ditch effort to change some votes in the Senate, their lobbying team took out a full-page newspaper advertisement urging Blue Cross patrons around the state to telephone the Senate's switchboard and private office numbers.

Within hours of the ad hitting the street, the Senate switchboard and private office numbers lit up to the point of blowing a fuse of some kind. The entire phone system locked up. I had to call in telephone repair experts, and the situation became intolerable. One senator from south Arkansas was unable to receive an emergency phone call about his father, who had had a fatal heart attack.

I was asked by Mike Beebe to find out who was responsible for the faux pas, and I promptly told him I knew just the man to call—Dr. George Mitchell, the president of Blue Cross, who just happened to be an old family friend from Sheridan.

I briefed Dr. Mitchell on what had happened, and he moved quickly, first sending letters of apology and making personal phone calls to senators. His next move was to bring in John Greer from Texas to take over the company's lobbying effort with the Arkansas General Assembly.

I found this out a short time later. I was out of state for a national legislative meeting when I received a call in my hotel room. It was John Greer, and he said he had flown in for the national meeting and wanted to discuss the Arkansas Senate with me over dinner. The two of us met, and coincidentally, each of us ordered the steak Diane as we settled in to talk Arkansas politics. We became great friends, and the friendship lasted through the years, even when health issues put the two of us on the sidelines. And he proved to be the ultimate lobbying pro, much like Cecil Alexander at Entergy, and he straightened out Big Blue's lobbying problems in a hurry by assembling an effective team whose members carried big checkbooks.

CHAPTER 18

As time marched on, I dealt less and less with members of the House after joining the Senate in 1985. But I did have one unpleasant encounter one evening with some of my old bosses who were *caught* once again with a greedy hand in the cookie jar.

As Bill Clinton prepared for his first term as president, Little Rock was preparing for its own huge inaugural gala. Thousands of people were coming to Little Rock for swanky downtown parties, and Arkansans were excited beyond their wildest dreams, and we all knew we were living history.

A week before the big night, I went to lunch with Senator Bud Canada and phone company lobbyist Skip Holland. Canada, a kind, caring legislator from Hot Springs, was very close to Clinton, and he was excited about the presidential parties that were being planned. He asked if it might be possible to establish a central gathering place for state legislators on the evening of the big parties so that transportation to and from the capitol to downtown events could be arranged.

I liked the idea and threw out some other suggestions over lunch. Bud asked Skip and me to coordinate the project, and we went to work immediately. Our plan was to use the Capitol Hill apartment building as a central headquarters where local representatives and senators could congregate, grab a refreshment, and then shuttle downtown to social events. Holland said he and other lobbyists would buy the food and drinks and have everything ready to serve at the apartment building lobby beginning at 6:00 p.m.

"I'm not opening the doors until straight up six o'clock," he insisted as we finalized the details. "If I open any sooner than that, we won't have anything left when most of the crowd arrives."

I liked the plan, and I left late in the afternoon to change clothes. Holland said he would set up the buffet and have everything ready on time.

But we overlooked one important detail. We forgot that several House members lived in the building and had apartments upstairs, within striking distance, so to speak, of the tempting buffet, which featured huge gulf shrimp.

I arrived back at the building at 5:45 p.m. and entered through a rear door. I walked into the reception area only to be confronted immediately by a fuming Holland, who was angry and red-faced.

"What's wrong?" I asked.

"They raided us. They took all the shrimp and carried it off!" he yelled pointing toward the elevator that accessed the upstairs apartments.

"Who took it?" I asked.

"Lacy and the rest of them," he said, accusing House member Lacy Landers and other House members who had apparently sniffed out the free food.

Holland calmed down long enough to explain how he had left the building momentarily to retrieve some articles from his car only to return to see the House members escaping with plastic bags full of shrimp they had taken from the buffet. He said they took the shrimp and put it in their freezers upstairs.

"Hey, I'll go get it," I said.

"You can't do that," he argued, trying to be a friend.

"Yes, I can, and I will," I said.

"No, I've already sent for more," he said.

"I don't care," I continued. "They shouldn't have done that, and maybe they were just playing a joke on you."

I went upstairs and asked the three men to please return the food, that guests for the presidential party were expected momentarily. One of them said they were only playing a joke on Holland, but I never believed the story. And after waiting almost an hour downstairs and staring at the elevator, I left for one of the big parties downtown. They never returned the shrimp, which cost the lobbyists more than $600.

Another story about House members and their petty desires involves Jim Holland, an accomplished representative from Knobel. He was a school principal and had the good looks of a Hollywood actor. But like his colleagues, he loved free handouts, and Tim Massanelli told one of the best stories ever about an encounter with the likable man we called Hollywood.

Massanelli said he was in his little office late one afternoon when Holland politely knocked and asked to go in. Holland hardly ever talked above a whisper, and I often referred to him as Whispering Jim. He had a gravelly growl in his voice, which made it more distinctive too. Massanelli, like the rest of us, enjoyed being around Holland because he was a likable, knowledgeable man. Massanelli waved him in and asked him what he could do for him.

"Hey, Tim, I was wondering if I might talk with you in private for a minute," he began.

Sensing something might be amiss, Massanelli rose to his feet and slowly closed the door so the two of them could talk.

"What is it?" Massanelli began.

"Uh, well, I wanted to see if you might do me a little favor," Holland opened up.

"I'll see," Massanelli said.

"Well, it's kinda private, and I'd like to keep it that way," Holland said, reaching inside his plaid sports coat.

Massanelli had no idea where the conversation was headed as Holland withdrew a Sharpie marking ink pen.

"See this pen?" Holland asked, raising the pen close to Massanelli.

"Yeah," Massanelli said.

"Well, uh, I was wondering if you might get me five or six more of these or maybe a box of 'em to take home."

Massanelli said he drew a deep breath and then answered.

"Dammit, Hollywood, I thought something was wrong with you, your health or something."

"Naw, I just want some of these ink pens."

"Yeah," Massanelli said. "I'll get you all the pens you want."

Many of the House members were intimidated by Massanelli, who had a tough Italian demeanor. His influence became even stronger as the House members became less and less experienced. After I went to the Senate, the senators were very receptive to new ideas and new technology that made their jobs easier, but Massanelli was resistant to change in the House, and this frustrated members there who were seeing the Senate trying new, innovative things.

This culminated one session when four House members came to visit me in my Senate office. They had heard the Senate was experimenting with a color copier, a new fax machine, and were looking at Senator David Malone's laptop computer as a possible new item for all senators in the future. I asked them the reason for their visit to my office.

"We want to see your new fax machine," Representative James Dietz told me. "We want to get one in the House, but Tim won't let us have one."

I was amazed at what I was hearing, but I understood their frustration. Dietz went on to say that the House members were organizing and planning to draft a bill ordering Massanelli to purchase a House fax machine.

"Don't do that," I urged Dietz. "Let me go talk to Tim first. He's just a little freaked out by any kind of technology that he thinks threatens the traditional way of doing business."

Turns out that Massanelli had expressed a concern that if the House installed a fax machine, the House members might choose to start phoning in their votes rather than attending the daily sessions. Dietz and his friends finally convinced Massanelli that his fears were unfounded, and the House got its very own fax machine.

Soon thereafter, the Senate ordered new personal computers for all its members, and the Arkansas Senate joined the Indiana Senate as the first two state legislative bodies in the nation to be "computerized." This set off another wave of protest in the House, and things really got testy when I announced that we were looking at digital photography.

CHAPTER 19

We all have our favorite Bill Clinton stories, about working with him and spending precious private moments. But I'll talk here about three of my own.

One occurred shortly after his gubernatorial defeat in 1980. Most of the state was in shock over Frank White's victory, and I was one of them—although all of us could see the race tightening in the final stretch. I dropped the young governor a personal note, and as he was packing up on the second floor of the capitol, he took time to jot down an answer, which I appreciated and kept as a favorite memento. The handwritten note was dated November 19, 1980, and it said: "Dear Bill. I'm grateful for your friendship and your counsel. Thanks. We'll have another day. Best, Bill."

My favorite memory of him was when he was elected president and the whirlwind of activity that followed at our own state capitol in Little Rock. After the parties and after the shock of him actually winning, it became time for him to actually depart.

This meant him going by the Senate offices for a private moment or two with some of the senators and me. It was an unbelievable experience to be a part of this fond farewell because so many of us had been with him from the start at the capitol, and now we were seeing him leave for the ultimate big stage. My heart swelled with pride as an Arkansan and a full-fledged Clinton supporter who admired him for so many reasons.

I got word that he would arrive at our offices in about fifteen minutes, so I gathered some of the senators together a few feet outside my office on the third floor, adjacent to the big Senate chamber. He arrived with Secret Service agents in tow, and the hugs and handshakes and reminiscing began in earnest. It was so hard to see him in this new "light," and I made the mistake of telling him, "You really do look different."

He countered, "Oh, don't say that."

But he *did* look different, and it's hard to explain it. Maybe it was the weight of the world already coming down on his shoulders, but he strolled among us, talking about journeys beginning and journeys ending. The photographers snapped our photos together, and the conversation was really going strong when one of the Secret Service agents, standing by the door at my office, walked up and interrupted. He asked the new president-elect to step aside with him, to my office, to take a phone call.

"I'll be with you in a minute," Clinton told the agent.

"Well, sir, it needs to be now."

A puzzled look came across his face, and the two men stepped away into my little office only a few feet away where Clinton was told a phone call awaited . . . on my phone!

After a short time, Clinton emerged, and I asked him if everything was all right.

"Yeah," he said. "You want to know who that was . . . it was Mikhail Gorbachev calling."

On my phone, no less. It hit me full bore. Things had really changed, not just for our new president, but for all of us.

One other Clinton story involves the president's last official visit to our state capitol. Mike Beebe was the Senate's pro tem, and Representative Shane Broadway of Bryant, a Beebe disciple, was the speaker of the House. Clinton wanted to visit his home state's capitol one more time before stepping down in Washington, and Beebe and Broadway devised the perfect plan. Mr. Clinton would address a joint session of the Arkansas legislature, just as he had done twenty years earlier as the young governor.

Arranging a presidential visit is a nightmare for all those involved in the preparations. In this instance, most of that responsibility fell on me and Massanelli. Mr. Clinton would address the 135 legislators and guests in the House chamber, and Massanelli and I would make all the arrangements. This meant working with Secret Service agents, securing the chamber and adjoining spaces, and rounding up all the information required, including social security numbers, birth dates, and any other pertinent data regarding those in attendance.

We met with the advance teams several times and made the changes they suggested. We also had to prepare a list of invited guests who would be near the president. The speaker could invite fifty guests, and so could the president pro tem. Beebe turned his part of the task over to me and said I should start keeping list of everyone who called who wanted to attend the joint session.

As the time drew near, I met with Beebe and said I had received several dozen requests for VIP passes. He asked me who had called, and I showed him the list, which included several "prominent" Arkansans, including Bill Bowen, the prominent banker and law dean who had served Clinton at the state level as chief of staff, and Paul Greenberg, the editorial writer for the *Arkansas Democrat-Gazette*. Both Bowen and Greenberg were friends of mine, and they were among twenty-four people who had called about possibly having a seat. I explained to Beebe that twenty-six other slots were available, but no one had requested them. The Senate staff and others who worked in the capitol were content to sit in a room downstairs from the House chamber where Clinton planned a walk through following his speech, so there was no rush to claim the VIP seating reserved for the Senate.

Beebe was satisfied with the plan, and I thought everything was going well. As requested, I sent my list of names to the Secret Service and forwarded a copy of my twenty-four invited guests to Massanelli in case some of the same people had contacted him for a seat.

A short time later, my phone rang, and it was Massanelli. He was fuming over some of the names on my list. He let loose with a stream of profanity and said it was "typical" of the Senate to use its invitation list to seat "big shots."

"Hell, Scoop," he began, "we could have invited Bill Bowen and Paul Greenberg, but we saved our fifty seats for our staff."

"Hey, Tim," I fired back, "that's fine, you do what you want to do, but our staff didn't want the seats, and you're welcome to our twenty-six seats we didn't fill."

He began to calm down as I explained further that the Senate staff was content to visit with Clinton in one of the legislative committee rooms following the speech. I said Bowen and Greenberg had phoned, and each man had politely asked if they might have a seat and that I kept a list for Beebe to show the order in which the calls were received.

We ended our conversation on a positive, friendly note, and I thought it was over until Beebe walked in. I explained what had happened, and he snapped his fingers and said, "Let's go."

"Go where?" I asked.

"To see Shane," he said as he whirled toward my door.

We walked briskly to the north end off the building and directly into the speaker's office. Broadway was seated at his desk, and Massanelli was standing next to him. Broadway's wife, Debbie, was standing in the room and greeted Beebe with a friendly hello.

"You need to leave," Beebe said sharply to the woman, and she quickly departed. Beebe asked Broadway if he had a problem with the way the Senate was handling the seating, and Broadway meekly replied that he did not. It ended almost as quickly as it blew up, but it demonstrated once again how the House suspected the Senate of high-handedness.

CHAPTER 20

T he Clinton visit for his swan-song speech to the legislature ended well and came off without a hitch. Beebe even spent some private time with the president to discuss a presidential pardon for an old political ally. The president also spent a few minutes with Les Wyatt, president of Arkansas State University, and it was a meeting I helped arrange. The university president and his lobbyist, Robert Evans, had asked me if there would be any possibility of meeting with the president to discuss a potential program that would benefit the Jonesboro institution.

The meeting happened, and Dr. Wyatt and Evans dropped by my office afterward to thank me for my assistance. Wyatt was so ingratiated that he asked if he might take me to dinner. I told him that I probably would be eating with Beebe and some of the senators, and he asked if they might want to join us. A new restaurant had opened on Chenal Parkway, and he wanted to check it out.

I asked Dr. Wyatt and Evans to walk with me to the west wing of the Senate, where Beebe had his pro tem office. I told them to wait outside and I would check with the other senators about the dinner invitation. Little did I realize how tired I was at that point and how the weeks of preparation had taken a toll on my nerves, not to mention a lack of sleep and the drain of working with the Secret Service gurus.

I walked in, and Beebe was sitting behind his big desk with his feet propped up. Several Senate colleagues, including Cliff Hoofman, Jon Fitch, and Jim Hill, were seated close by.

"Great job, Scoop," Beebe opened up to me. "Y'all did a great job, and it was a great day for all of us, the president included."

"I think everything went well," I answered. "Hey, Dr. Wyatt and Robert Evans are out here, and they're offering to take us, all of us here, to dinner if you're up to it."

"What's the deal?" Beebe asked.

"Well, I did them a little favor today, and they're happy with the way things turned out, and now they're hungry, and Dr. Wyatt read about a new restaurant out by Chenal Country Club."

"Sounds great," Beebe said. "When we goin'?"

"I'm ready now, if y'all are."

"Where is this place you said out on Chenal?" Jim Hill asked.

"I'm not sure, Senator, but it's in a little shopping center about a mile before you get to the golf course, on the right," I answered.

"How far out there is that?" Fitch asked.

"Hey, Jon, I don't know how far it is, I'm just here to ask," I answered.

"Well, fine, you don't have to bite my head off," he said.

"Hey, I'm not doing any biting here. I'm just passing along a dinner invitation."

"They're havin' a big dinner down at the hotel downtown tonight too," Hoofman offered.

"Yeah, that's on the social calendar we passed out," I said.

"Hey, do you want to go to dinner, Scoop?" Beebe interrupted.

"To be honest, Senator, I wanna go home and put my fuckin' feet up and rest," I said sharply.

"Whew," Hill said, laughing and throwing his hands in the air.

"Hey, look. I came in here, two men are waiting outside ready to buy you a free meal, you may have to get in your fancy cars and drive five or six miles, but that's the deal, take it or leave it," I said, as mad and disgusted as I had ever been with these men who were my bosses and my friends.

"Why don't you tell them thanks but that we'll do it another time," Beebe said.

I left the room, and Dr. Wyatt was gracious and understanding. He thanked me again for my help and said he would always remember me for the way I had helped him and the university. I thought a minute about Max Howell's elk and Wyatt's predecessor and how I had heard similar words before from the Arkansas State brass.

After our blowout in Beebe's office, I walked back across the hall to my office to prepare to head home. I looked up, and Hoofman was standing in my doorway. "Hey, I'm sorry about all of that over there. We don't act very senatorial at times," he said.

"That's okay, Cliff. I'm tired, and you guys, well, sometimes I get a little frustrated, that's all."

"The dinner downtown tonight at the hotel, is that just for House members, or can senators attend too?" he asked me.

"It's for the House, but no one will care if you come. I'll call the guy who's in charge and ask him."

Hoofman left and walked a few feet away to his office. I made the call and found out that all legislators were invited. I shouted out to Hoofman across the hall, and he said "Thanks."

Minutes later, Jon Fitch walked in. "Well, are you cooled off?" he said, smiling a sheepish smile.

"Yeah, but man, Jon, y'all can act like a bunch of spoiled kids sometimes," I said.

"That's because we are a bunch of spoiled kids."

"You got that right."

"The dinner downtown, are senators invited . . ."

"Yes," I interrupted. "Cliff asked me, and I made a call down there, and you and your wife can go."

"Well, sounds like the House staff did a heck of a job preparing a big dinner," he said, trying to jab me one last time.

"Yeah," I answered jabbing back, "they're doing a lot better job over in the House now that you got your sorry, fat ass out of there."

We laughed all the way to the car. He went to the dinner, and I went home to rest my weary bones.

I thought all the way home about the good relationship I had with some of the senators. We were like brothers, like the men in the movie *The Sting*, a comparison I would make to Beebe, who liked my observation so much we developed our own secret signal, known only to Beebe's men, those in the secret Worm Club. In the movie, the men who were setting up the secret sting would communicate to one another by touching the side of their nose with their finger, a club salute as it were. I showed this to Beebe, and it was the sign we adopted when we wanted to signal to each other in secret. It was a childish gesture, perhaps, but it was a lot of fun, and politics can be a lot of fun when people forget about taking themselves too seriously, a rarity on most days, for sure.

Being with Clinton again reminded me of his amazing presence, the way heads turned when he entered a room. This disarming charisma served him well although it led to some of his well-known dalliances. But a lot of people I worked with at the state capitol were extremely loyal to him and his wife, and they worked their tails off in his presidential races, fully aware of his insatiable desire to move up the political ladder.

Like so many, I was never reluctant to speak up on his behalf, and on two occasions, this led to public outbursts I look back on with some regret. The first occurred during his first run for the presidency. I was asked to attend a surprise birthday party at Cajun's Wharf, a popular Little Rock restaurant. We gathered at four thirty in the afternoon, and it was a group of about twenty people, all strangers to me except the young lady who had accompanied me. After settling in, I struck up a very pleasant conversation with a local physician who practiced at the University of Arkansas Medical Sciences campus. He said he had seen me at the capitol, and we talked over a number of things, including Clinton's just-announced run for the White House.

A man sitting across me interrupted and asked, "So you like Bill Clinton?" Naturally, I could tell from the tone he was not a Clinton fan.

"Well, yes, I do," I answered.

"All he's ever done is raise taxes," the man fired back, getting more agitated as he spoke.

"Well, I guess taxes are a necessary way of life, just ask the doctor here who works at the Med Center, which your taxes helped build."

"Is that right?" he continued. "Well, I guess you're just like Clinton?"

"Let me ask you something," I came back. "Did you drive up here today, to the restaurant?"

"Yeah, so what?"

"Well, the highway that you drove on was possible because of taxes," I countered.

"Yeah, so what?"

"Are you a parent?" I asked, with him answering that he had two kids who attended school.

"What do you think pays for the school bus to pick up your kids, and what do you think pays for the teachers to teach your kids to read and write—taxes do!" I said, starting to raise my voice.

"What else, Mr. Big Shot?" he asked.

"Well, are your parents still living?" I asked.

"My dad died, but my mom's in the nursing home."

"Well, what do you think helps pay the people who feed and take care of your mother? Taxes," I said, trying to wind down and keep my blood pressure under control.

At this point, he turned beet red and moved back in his chair. "Well, let's just go outside and settle this," he said.

I told him I had rather leave it where it stood, and my date and I left, not bothering to look back and not bothering to stay for a piece of the delicious-looking chocolate birthday cake.

The other story concerns Hillary, and it occurred during her service as secretary of state. Another Arkansan—this one an elderly lady— had no compunction in expressing her dislike for Hillary and her boss, President Obama. I was seated in a doctor's office in Little Rock, alone for almost a half hour, until the door opened and an elderly woman and her husband entered. She signed her name on the patient sign-in sheet and then instructed her mousy husband to take a seat.

I sat near them, quietly reading a *Good Housekeeping* magazine, waiting my call to go back to another room to see the doctor. A nurse walked in and asked the elderly woman if she had signed the sign-in sheet. She said yes and then asked the young nurse, "What do you think about this Obamacare, the court ruling?"

The nurse was reluctant to talk, but the woman pressed on. Finally, the nurse took the middle ground and said, "Well, no doubt it will mean a change in the way a lot of doctors do business."

I thought it was a very diplomatic answer, but it didn't satisfy the questioner. "Huh," she gruffed, "they need to get rid of Obama. He's nothing but a socialist."

Of course, everyone had heard this accusation before, and I just accepted it and kept quiet. But she was not finished, and she apparently was confident that more editorial comment was needed. This was when she directed her attention to the large TV on the wall, which was showing Hillary exiting a plane in some foreign country. "And there's another one we need to get rid of somehow—she ain't no good."

I had heard enough, and my blood began to boil. I folded my magazine and put it down. Then I turned to the woman, seated only a few feet away.

"Why in the world would you say such awful things about people?" I started in.

"Well, you know what I mean," she answered.

"No, ma'am, I don't know what you mean. First, I doubt that you can even spell the word *socialist*, and I'll bet my last dollar you have never read one word about what the health-care plan will actually do, and secondly, and I hope to God you hear me because I've had to sit here and listen to you, but you ought to get down on your knees every night and thank the good Lord for Hillary Clinton because she opened a lot of doors for you and every other woman, not just in this country, but in countries around the world."

By this time, my voice was elevated, and her husband was getting nervous. "Well, I think this has gone far enough," he volunteered.

"I agree, but your wife opened all of this up, and she needs to tone her unsolicited opinions down in a public place, especially a doctor's office, where people are sick and need peace and quiet."

At this point, the nurse raced in and called me back. As I walked away, I turned one more time, looked at the woman, and said, "I deplore ignorance!"

Some time later, I asked my buddy Skip Rutherford, a Clinton loyalist, if Bill and Hillary actually knew how adamant their friends really were in standing up for them. "I think they do, Scoop," he said, laughing about my doctor's office story.

CHAPTER 21

T he Worm Club and its genesis seem to be a point of some dispute each Christmas when we gather for a Worm Club dinner. After Beebe became governor, Ron Maxwell, the very capable social director at the Governor's Mansion, phoned me to inquire about a possible Christmas dinner for Beebe's close friends. The governor had asked Maxwell to contact me about planning the dinner and told Maxwell I would know who would be on the Worm Club list of invitees.

The Worm Club was born one evening at a Little Rock restaurant. Beebe and his close Senate associates were having dinner and celebrating a major Nick Wilson defeat. Earlier in the day, Wilson had seen Beebe and his charges successfully dismantle a long-established Wilson program that guaranteed Wilson power and prestige. It was a major defeat for Wilson and signaled the start of the powerful senator's demise in the legislature. It meant that Beebe and his men were solidly in control of Arkansas politics and that the sky was the limit for the young Democratic leader from Searcy who was becoming everyone's shining star.

As we finished off dinner and each of Beebe's disciples recounted the day's events, various attendees, including some Republicans, rose to toast the occasion. Finally, Paul Berry, a brilliant, effusive tactician and longtime political kingmaker who had turned to lobbying for a profession, rose to toast Beebe and his men. It was a decision-turning day for Berry, who had been a Wilson ally, but he had turned over a new leaf in the wake of Wilson's defeat to be among Beebe's clan this evening.

Berry, also a close friend of mine from previous political campaigns, was stealing the evening with his humorous one-liners, and we anxiously awaited his promised toast as he asked permission from the group to rise and acknowledge the importance of the day.

He slowly lifted his wineglass and spoke eloquently, looking angelically to the ceiling: "What was vouchsafed was foresworn," he said at one point, everyone nodding in agreement as we tried our best to understand the meaning of his obtuse toast—some remote reference I thought to Walt Whitman or a Catholic doctrine or some ancient poem he had studied years earlier at college. I was sitting next to him as he spoke, slowly sipping my tequila as I studied his animated antics. He seemed to be on a roll, but he suddenly stopped as his words became incomprehensible. Sensing that my old friend needed help, I clutched my tequila bottle with the funny, fat worm on the label, stood before the group, and proclaimed in my best theatrical voice, "To the worm!"

Everyone stood in unison and shouted, "To the worm!"

And thus, a tradition was born. It made no sense whatsoever, but the worm became our rallying cry, our motto, our boyish frat-house way of bonding in the name of good government. We would relive the dinner in our later years and try to recall everything that happened at that historic gathering—who was there, what all was said, and how the rambling Berry toast led to the climactic declaration. Some say Senator Mike Everett might have said something that influenced the worm reference, but none of us have perfect recollection of the event, which is certainly understandable.

In the years that followed, we had other Senate dinners and quietly inducted new members into the club, even some who came along after the term limits amendment began in earnest. But it was never the same with the new members. They didn't understand the "real Senate" that we had nurtured, nor did they understand the vicious wars that had been fought with Max Howell and Knox Nelson and Nick Wilson, the ups and downs of everyday existence, the byzantine deals and cozy arrangements, the scheming factions that kept everyone on constant watch. This new, green bunch of rookies would have no institutional memory to fortify them, no bond that rallied them to good government causes, no craving to sit at happy hour with their friends and talk about hopes and dreams. The old pros were gradually walking toward the exits, and there were damned few of us left to watch over this beautiful place that had caused us absolute grief and joy at the same time. The Arkansas Senate that we knew—that ol' Max knew, that hundreds of experienced old tigers had known—was closing down, its system on life support, a tragic victim of voter distrust and Republican think tanks, understandably crippled and finally fatally wounded by arrogance and distrust.

CHAPTER 22

As Mike Beebe took office as governor, a reporter asked me if I could name the people from bygone Senate days who were really close to him. I deferred and said that would be the new governor's call if he wanted to *out* his political lieutenants, his inner circle, his kitchen cabinet. But that was then—and now, some time has passed, and sitting at the computer, in the peace and quiet of retirement, I am comfortable in naming some of those people. And in order to do so, I wouldn't have to look very far from the Worm Club table. Some of these people are called his "buddy pals," a term given him by Rocky Willmuth of Batesville, one of those who pulled up a chair at the Worm Club dinner table. Some listed are not Worm Clubbers but are Beebe disciples nonetheless.

To start the list, I'll list the legislators. Morril Harriman of Van Buren would be at the top. Beebe's meteoric rise to power in the Senate might have happened without Harriman, but it is doubtful. A shrewd lawyer, Harriman was close to Nick Wilson when he started his Senate career, but he soon migrated to Beebe's team and became an integral part of the reform movement of the 1990s. Throw in Cliff Hoofman of North Little Rock, another of Beebe's lawyer friends who despised Wilson, and the late Jon Fitch of Hindsville, a fiery cattle farmer who brought a huge dose of common sense to the cause. Add David Malone of Fayetteville, the quiet, scholarly law professor, and Steve Bell, the ever-steady lawyer from Batesville—and you have some of the magical ingredients that helped Beebe formulate his recipe for change. Later, Bill Gwatney, a spunky upstart who replaced the aging

Max Howell, gave incredible energy and frankness to the cause, and they were aided in their reform efforts by Tom Kennedy, Jim Hill, Percy Malone, John Riggs, Vic Snyder, Jay Bradford, and a few others. As I said earlier, Bradford's stunning victory over Knox Nelson after a reapportionment shake-up was perhaps the most dynamic game changer in the history of Arkansas politics. Everything, everything changed when Nelson went down as Max Howell, sensing the glory days were over, announced a month later that he was stepping down too. The announcement came days after the brash Bradford made a civic club speech in Howell's very own Senate district and encouraged voters in Howell's district to get rid of the aging senator. It was the boldest move I had ever seen in state politics, and it accomplished exactly what Bradford intended—it scared the hell out of Howell and forced him to step down.

As Beebe's numbers grew, he looked to Lu Hardin, Charlie Cole Chaffin, Mike Everett, and others to increase his standing. We were on a roll, and he confided in me about his plans. Term limits had not even entered the picture, and Mike Beebe contemplated a long, long career in the Arkansas Senate, the place he loved more than anything. His team was consumed with energy, planning and scheming every day and night, over lunch, at happy hour, over evening meals with favorite lobbyists who were also on board with the new movement.

I was thrilled to be the nonlegislator member of the group and the person who organized our time together. The "straw that stirred the drink," as Don Tilton called me. Other members included Tilton, Beebe's cagey constant companion who had locked on to Beebe early. Tilton had been in an executive position with Arkansas State, and his legislative prowess became legendary at the Jonesboro campus about the time Beebe won election to the Senate. Other lobbyists who were close to the group included the wily old pro Cecil Alexander, phone company exec Eddie Drilling, independent lobbyist Paul Berry, and the consummate gentleman John Greer of Blue Cross Blue Shield. Others who accompanied the group from time to time were Carey Baskin of Alltel and Phil Matthews with the Hospital Association. These were frequent guests at the Beebe gatherings, but there were dozens of other lobbyists too who swarmed the group for attention, always ready to pick up the tab for dinner and drinks.

If you were out on the town in Little Rock, you could find us at our favorite haunts—Buster's, the Afterthought, Doe's, or a late-night breakfast spot. House members were bunched up at lobbyist-sponsored buffets, while Beebe's group ate at the finest restaurants and sipped fine wines from the wine lists they studied in their spare time.

We traveled together to the finest golf courses, in lobbyist-owned private jets, and we did everything together. We were burning every candle we could scrape together at both ends and loving every minute of it, even when it drained all our energy. Legislative sessions were long and arduous, but they were fun and exciting and productive—not just for special interests that always dominate the political scene, but for good government causes too. Our Senate finances were straightened out, and our money, all the public's money, was accounted for by newly hired accountants and state auditors who were allowed to inspect our books.

I was proud of the work we were doing, and the things we were doing as a staff were being noticed not only at the capitol but also by others around the country. I was asked to speak at legislative meetings in other states, and I was invited by two other states to set up programs identical to the ones I started in Arkansas. As things improved and I advanced up the ranks, I gained a lot of self-confidence. I knew we had established a gold standard of excellence at the Senate, and I was very proud of the work product. Some nights, alone at the Senate, I would walk out into the huge chamber, which was still and quiet, and think about how I had made my career moves. I had come a long way from the sports reporter job at the *Pine Bluff Commercial*, my first career stop, and I was very happy watching over this big place. I wanted the very best for the Arkansas Senate, and I was convinced all the pieces of the puzzle we had envisioned as a team had fallen neatly into place.

On the other side, it was becoming serious for Wilson and his declining numbers. I received a phone call from a big-time lobbyist who asked if I'd like to go to grab some barbecue for lunch, a favorite treat of mine. I gladly accepted the invitation because I liked the man, and I respected his opinion a great deal since he had been a part of the political scene for several generations.

As we rode in his car to the restaurant, he opened up about the Beebe-Wilson conflict that was clearly out in the open. "I don't know how you feel about all of that, and I know you are in a sensitive position, but I'm betting my money on Nick Wilson," the man said, a statement I thought rather odd since we had barely started our car ride.

"That's your business," I said back to him.

"Well, I know you're close to Beebe, but I never would sell Nick Wilson short," he continued.

"Well, if we're talking about people not coming up short, I'd bet money on Mike Beebe before I'd bet on anybody else," I said.

"Well, we'll see," he said.

We had a nice lunch, but I never went to lunch with the man again. I knew why he had called, and the reason was obvious: he wanted me on Nick's team and not with Beebe. I knew he was wrong that day, and I knew it later on too, when Nick Wilson, a brilliant man, foolishly and carelessly went overboard on a controversial issue and ended up in prison. Mike Beebe, on the other hand, ended up in the Governor's Mansion. The lobbyist? He lost his job with his big client, about the time Wilson went away to the big house.

Another well-known and successful lobbyist cornered me late one night at the Afterthought bar. He was very inebriated, but he insisted we talk for a few minutes. I had known the man for years, first seeing him as a member of the House of Representatives. I considered him a friend, and I had attended legislative functions in his home, but I also knew he was a Nick Wilson loyalist who had not been close to Mike Beebe.

In the corner of the small jazz bar, he insisted we talk, so I agreed to some private time. "I just want you to know how sorry I am," he began, slurring his words as he attempted to stand erect, "about being so close to Nick and everything, but I have to do what I have to do."

"You don't owe me any explanation about your work," I assured him.

"But I do," he kept on. "I'm just telling you as an old friend that I admire the work y'all are doing, you and Beebe, even though I'm seeing it from the other side, you know."

I told him I appreciated his frankness, and I never repeated anything he said that evening. I'm not sure he remembered any of it anyway, but I could tell he was feeling some remorse over decisions he had made in his life. But who doesn't do that from time to time? I reasoned. After that, we never spoke again, but I certainly held no grudges.

CHAPTER 23

And about Nick Wilson. He became the poster boy, of course, for the term limits argument. It seemed every editorial writer invoked his sullied name when they argued for term limiting legislators, and who could blame them? But Nick Wilson's career ended because a piece of good legislation went sour. So in retrospect, as I look back over my career, I smile occasionally when I think of Nick Wilson because he was a brilliant and skilled politician. He and his old friend Bill Walmsley, the senator from Batesville, were an awesome team in their early years in the Senate, actual reformers who were fighting the scheming against Max Howell, Mutt Jones, and Knox Nelson.

I too have good memories of working with Wilson, some of which I related earlier in the text here, especially in my wars with Max Howell. I will say this: in my role as chief of staff, I never, ever went to Wilson with an issue and was turned away or treated unfairly. In fact, he always delivered on what I asked.

Of course, I realize he might have been a very happy man had he gathered the majority vote in the Senate and saw to it that I went away. I realized that then and I realize that now, but that is the nature of the beast. I was on the winning side, and I was proud to be associated with the team that won the Beebe-Wilson war.

On a lighter note, I will relate one funny Nick Wilson story. Well, maybe a couple because the man had a wonderful sense of humor.

He phoned me one afternoon and asked me to step across the Senate chamber to visit in his office. He said he had an "interesting story" to tell me.

The story concerned a female office holder who had offices in the capitol. The woman had been around for a while, and she had some unusual habits, including her strong belief in psychics and ghostly things. She even had an assistant who read tea leaves and made predictions to her about her "political enemies," of which I was one she considered to be among her worst.

I didn't have time to worry about what the woman was doing, and I certainly never set out to do her any political harm, but she believed what she wanted to believe, and that was her business.

Anyway, we were in the middle of a legislative session, and the woman's office budget was being held up in the Joint Budget Committee. She had told people in and around the capitol that Senator Jodie Mahony and I were the culprits and that the two of us were using pressure on others to hold up her budget. And this was what she told Wilson after she asked him to walk down to her office for a one-on-one visit.

Well, the meeting didn't go as planned, and that was what Wilson was phoning me about. I walked into Nick's office, and he was laughing and smoking one of his big cigars. "Sit down," he said, pointing to one of his well-upholstered chairs. "I got a story you'll appreciate and you sure won't believe."

"About what?" I asked, then pausing long enough for him to call her name. "What has she done now?" I asked.

"Well," Nick begins, "I get this phone call from her, asking me if I'll come down and talk privately with her about her budget. She's saying you and Jodie are jacking her around or something, and I told her I'd be happy to come down and talk."

Wilson went on to explain that he walked into the woman's office, and the two of them stepped inside her inner office, just the two of them.

"Now, we're sitting there, and she's, like, half-ass whispering. Now, you remember who Bruce Bennett was, right, back a few years ago?"

Nodding my head in the affirmative, I was wondering at this point what Bruce Bennett, the former state attorney general, had to do with this story.

"Well, we're sitting there, and we're talking about how to get her budget moving, and this little puff of smoke or dust falls out of the air-conditioning vent a few feet above her head. Well, all of a sudden, she stops talking and waves for me to be quiet and to step outside, out of her office. We walk outside, and I ask her what's going on, and she says, 'We can't talk in there. Bruce Bennett's ghost is in there, and he's listening to what we're sayin'.'"

I couldn't believe what the senator was telling me, and we were both in stitches laughing about all this. Nick continued, "I looked at her and said, 'Dammit, don't call me again,' and I walked off."

I had a longtime friend from Sheridan who worked for this woman. Even though it was a public office, I had to be careful about phoning him because the woman had instructed the office receptionist to log all incoming calls to employees so that she could review the call list at the end of each week, to see who had been calling the various departments. It was related to her intense paranoia, my friend told me.

But I had to make occasional calls, even knowing that the receptionist would ask for my name. So I adopted a plan of my own, not realizing that I should have informed my friend who was on the receiving end.

When I phoned, the receptionist would greet me and ask whom I was calling and then ask for my name. And I would tell her I was Lou Brock. I thought it was funny, and I knew the young receptionist would not recognize the name of the famous Arkansas ballplayer who achieved Hall of Fame status with the St. Louis Cardinals. After a short pause, she would patch the call through, and my friend would answer.

This went on for several months, and then one day, my friend was summoned to the big office by the big boss. He suspected that something was up, but he took a seat in front of his boss and let her start up.

"So," she began, "I want to ask you something—you want to tell me who this Lou Brock person is, who's calling you?"

Puzzled and not knowing what in the world had led his boss to begin with this question, he countered, "Everybody knows who Lou Brock is. He's the left fielder for the St. Louis Cardinals."

"The left fielder for the St. Louis Cardinals?" she asked back. "Well, you want to tell me why he's been calling you for the last three months?"

My friend told me the story later that day, and he was still laughing. "I told her it was just one of my crazy friends," he confessed.

"You didn't tell her it was me?" I asked.

"Hell no, she would have fired me," he said.

The Bruce Bennett ghost story was a favorite, and it was one of the best moments I spent with Nick Wilson. One other favorite Nick story was from early in my Senate career when Max and Knox were still competing for power and pitting Wilson and Beebe against each other so that they could keep the two young leaders apart. Nelson had seen me in Wilson's little office one day, and as I left, he motioned me to go see him. I walked only a few feet into Nelson's office, and Nelson promptly asked me what Nick wanted with me.

"We were just sharing a funny story or two," I told Nelson, not ready to divulge any part of my conversation with Wilson.

"You need to watch ol' Nick. He's sinister," Nelson advised.

Later that day, Wilson eased up to me on the Senate floor and asked me if Nelson had threatened me about being in his office. "No," I assured him.

"Well, what did he want?" Wilson asked. "Oh, he just told me that you were sinister," I told Wilson.

"Sinister." Wilson laughed. "I guess that old son of a bitch has been reading the dictionary again. He doesn't even know what *sinister* means."

Wilson was probably right, because Nelson did get confused about big words. My brother Bob wrote in a column that Nelson was "oleaginous," and Nelson cornered me later in the day after the article appeared and wanted to know what in the world my brother was implying. Then he asked me what the word meant, and I said it implied that he was "kind of oily and slick." This enraged the senator, and he instructed me, "Tell your brother that he is, well, he is, he is just shit." I think the senator understood the meaning of those words.

CHAPTER 24

I hit the ground running in June 1985 as the Senate's first chief of staff. My goal was to do what I had been doing in the House while gradually expanding services to the thirty-five senators who had been denied a lot of the staff services afforded their House colleagues. Ad agencies call this "branding," and that was my goal, to brand the Senate as the happening place in Arkansas politics. I knew Mike Beebe and the younger senators were becoming very popular with the media, so I wanted to build on this positive exposure. I expanded our publicity effort by offering a daily radio copy to each senator during legislative sessions and encouraging each of my bosses to phone in daily radio reports to their stations back home. I also ordered weekly newspaper columns written for the senators so that they could ask their local editors back home for space in their hometown newspapers. I had friendly relationships with some of the Little Rock columnists and would tip them from time to time about behind-the-scene activities, especially when it involved Beebe, who was growing in popularity. I also agreed to be an occasional on-air analyst for a Little Rock TV station, and this gave me a lot of leeway in talking about the Senate and the senators. Our staff services were expanded to include speech writing, press reports, legal services, and ethics compliance. I even had my janitor/property officer picking up and delivering senators to the airport to save them the trouble of parking their cars. I also had a speech schedule of my own, traveling to the senators' hometowns when they wanted me to speak to their civic clubs and school groups.

To appreciate where the new staff had to start in its work, all I had to do was reflect on my first day on the job at the Senate. I walked into the celebrated Senate Quiet Room, the big private lounge in the rear of the Senate chamber. The furniture needed polishing, the lime-green carpet needed cleaning, and in the very back of the room, in the kitchen area, a giant Coleman milk machine was unplugged and leaking spoiled milk. My janitor and I moved the machine away from the wall, and a swarm of giant roaches scrambled for cover. The machine had been unplugged for weeks, the milk had soured and leaked onto the floor, and no one had bothered to even clean up the mess. It was my first day on the job, and it signaled to me that I had a long way to go to get things done in a proper way.

As Beebe climbed the ladder, I sought more and more ways to get his name out. The *Farkleberry Follies*, the popular stage show at Murry's Dinner Theater, was being written, and I was working with my old newspaper boss Leroy Donald in scripting the production. We were searching desperately for a big show-stopper number, and we were coming up short on ideas.

I took a break from the writing and bought a couple of tickets for the *Les Misérables* production at Robinson Auditorium in Little Rock. It has always been one of my favorite shows, and I couldn't wait to hear the music again this night. As the actors sang, the tune resonated, and I reached for a pen and paper and began scribbling, knowing that I had found the perfect number for our *Follies* show. It would be entitled "Everybody Loves Mike Beebe," to the tune of "Master of the House" from *Les Misérables*.

Our show was a big hit in its weeklong run, and the Beebe tune, featuring my old acting friend Bill Glasscock as Mike Beebe, was dynamic. Beebe and his Senate pals sat on the front-row opening night, and he beamed as the local actors sang his praises and elevated him to star status. Mike Beebe was becoming a well-known name in Arkansas politics, and his future was limitless.

After Huckabee became governor, Beebe became his close legislative advisor. To advertise a popular new health program, Beebe teamed with Huckabee in a statewide public relations program that included public service announcements on TV. This broadened Beebe's image and showed his bipartisan approach to politics to a statewide audience.

During Beebe's last days at the Senate, he let it be known that he planned to run for attorney general. Some wanted him to go ahead and take a poke at the governor's race, but he politely declined, knowing that the AG's office was the perfect place to lay the groundwork for a future career in the higher office.

We talked about his departure from the Senate, and it was a poignant moment. We had come a long way together, and we had enjoyed enormous progress. Max and Knox and Nick were all gone, and the place was not the same. We were confident we had done a good job and that state government was on sound footing, even if we disagreed with a lot of Mike Huckabee's politics.

And the time came for me to discuss my future with him. He was quick and to the point, as usual, and said he would like for me to go with him to the AG's office and be his public spokesman. The job wouldn't pay quite as much as my Senate salary did, but it was mine if I wanted it. I told him that there was little doubt in my mind that I would gladly accept his offer and move downtown with him to his new offices.

A week later, however, Senator Jim Hill of Nashville walked into my office. He asked if I planned to play golf at Chenal Country Club the following day with two of our mutual friends, and I said yes, those were my plans. He said he would be joining us too and that he wanted me to ride with him in the golf cart.

The next day, we teed off, and on hole number 5, Hill opened up. He explained that he intended to be the next Senate pro tem and that he was unsure about his declining health and whether or not he really wanted to take on the added responsibilities. I assured him he could handle the job in his sleep, as good as he was with people.

"Well, that's what I wanted to talk to you about," he said.

"Okay," I answered.

"I'm not going to do this pro tem thing if you are leaving," he said to me.

"Come on, man," I said.

"No, really. I've talked to Beebe, and he said it's up to you, but if you'll stay at the Senate, stay with me for a while, I'll do this pro tem thing, and we'll have a lot of fun."

I'll always remember the conversation and the very spot on the beautiful golf course where we stopped the golf cart—hole number 5 on the Founders Course. I was humbled by his words, and I decided to stay for a while longer to help Hill as much as I could. I stayed long enough to see the renovation project through and see Hill become a respected, wise, and beloved leader. He was a joy to work with, and he was a very effective pro tem and leader of the legislature. I left in January 2004, about twenty-six years after signing on with John Miller and following Mr. Witt's lead, to move back home to a new job in Sheridan—running Mr. Witt's beautiful museum.

CHAPTER 25

I have to devote a little space to Senator Jay Bradford of Pine Bluff in discussing my work with the various pro tems. He was one of the last pro tems I worked with, and for the most part, Jay was pleasant and easygoing.

The Nick Wilson indictments were handed down during this time, and that led to a lot of work and tension. We broke a lot of new ground during that time, and none of it was easy, not even for those who despised Wilson and were glad to see him stripped of his committee chairmanship.

Bradford came under a lot of heat during that period for not pushing the Senate to act more promptly in stripping Wilson of some of his privileges following the indictment, but we were trying to be very careful during the investigation and interrogations that were taking place. After all, it wasn't really for any of us to judge Wilson—that would have to be left to the courts.

But in recalling that time, I'm reminded of an episode that impacted my relationship with Jay, which led to him circling back and asking for my help.

It was early in the session, and the senators were adjourning to walk to the north end of the building to hear the governor during his joint session address in the House chamber. I rarely attended these speeches because I had too much work to do, and on this day, I was dealing with a personnel problem involving a ninety-year-old sergeant at arms who worked under me.

The old man had worked for us for several years, but he was losing his memory, and he really had become a liability more than anything because he was unable to climb the stairs and pay attention in dealing with the duties of the job.

One of the constitutional officers, Treasurer Jimmie Lou Fisher, had called me the day before to say the man had shown up in her office and was handing out dimes and other small coins to young females in the office. She said he seemed addled and suggested I look into it.

The senators had all left to attend the joint session when I walked out of my office to step across the hall to the men's bathroom. Out in the hall, near the women's restroom, a channel 11 reporter was setting up her camera for an interview. I asked her what she was planning to shoot, and she said her station was doing a feature story on our ninety-year-old sergeant at arms. She said the man's family had phoned the station and suggested the news team do a feature on the old man.

I shook my head and walked on to the bathroom a few feet away. I opened the door, and standing inside the small tile-clad room was the very sergeant at arms we had been discussing. The sad and startling thing, however, was that he was standing in the room, naked and unaware of where he was. I shouted for him to get his clothes and get dressed, and I called another sergeant from outside the room for assistance. We sent the man home and away from the capitol as soon as we could.

I walked back across the hall and told the reporter there would be no story, that the Senate did not allow its employees, especially session employees, to be featured on the news. She exploded in a rage, packed her gear, and left for the station.

About an hour later, Senator Bradford, back from the House, roared into my office. "Bill, what's this about you telling channel 11 they can't film a story out here?" he screamed.

"That's exactly what I told them, Jay," I said.

"Man, you can't do that. You can't tell them what they can film and what they can't film."

"Yes, I can, and I've done it ever since I've been here. We have a rule about where they can film, and we don't put our employees, especially session employees, on the air."

"Mel Hanks, their director, is threatening to sue me," he continued.

"Then let him sue."

"Well, you can't do this."

"Then let's go see Beebe. He'll tell you different."

We hurried to Beebe's office across the hall and walked in. I explained what I had done, and Beebe, in his typical calm way, looked at Bradford and said, "Scoop's right. We don't film our employees."

Then I asked Jay to settle down and explained the whole situation. The next day, I asked my head sergeant to inform the old man that his services were no longer needed at the Senate. It was a sad situation, but the man obviously needed some kind of help that we didn't have available.

I say all this to bring up a second situation with Bradford. After the sergeant episode, the press got fired up a short time later about Nick Wilson and the expected criminal charges. Reporters were asking when the Senate would strip Wilson of some of his privileges, and one of the TV stations, channel 11, started following Bradford in and out of every committee room at the capitol. It was starting to unnerve him, and he finally came to me and said, "Hey, you gotta do something about channel 11—they're worrying the hell out of me."

Remembering the earlier episode and his statement about Mel Hanks and a threatened lawsuit, I smiled and said, "Sounds to me like you need to call your buddy Mel Hanks."

Jay laughed his patented laugh and walked off, waving a good-natured good-bye.

CHAPTER 26

With every job, in every profession, there is inside fun stuff. And we had plenty of inside fun stuff, funny stories to tell then and to this day. Reminiscing is half the fun as I look back on my time inside the legislature. I'll begin my favorite stories segment with Senator Jack Gibson, the roly-poly little senator from Boydell in Southeast Arkansas.

He was a gifted, athletic man who won acclaim as a fighter pilot in World War II. We talked a lot about his wartime experiences, the Japanese planes he remembered shooting down, his escape after being shot down himself in Tokyo Bay.

But it was his quick wit that endeared him to so many of us who had the privilege of working with him. He taught me how to drink vodka Cajun martinis, and we traveled around the country, attending meetings, playing golf, and talking. You could learn a lot from Jack Gibson, unlike a lot of other people in politics who only wanted to talk about themselves. I remember being in California, in the rich, fertile farming country, and I asked him a question about the huge irrigation sprinklers and watering the crops. We have these huge sprinklers in Arkansas too, and I asked Jack, who was a farmer and a banker, what powered the devices. He explained how they're hooked to water wells and pumps, but he also offered a bit more information. "As big as they are, they have a tiny, little metal washer on the end of the piping system, and without that little washer, the whole thing would shut down."

It wasn't a big deal, talking about the metal washer, but it told me a lot about the man, how he knew so much about so many things. He was as multidimensional as any person I ever knew. He could talk all night about farming or banking or gambling or women or politics or food or—oh, well, you get the picture.

But three stories come to mind when I think of my old friend, who had passed on. The first concerns Bill Clinton's plan to name Jack the new state banking commissioner. Jack was serving in the Senate and was very popular with everyone at the capitol. I was sitting in my office one afternoon, and he charged in, full of energy as usual, and said, "I'll be seeing you, Scoop."

I didn't think much about it and replied, "You headed home to Boydell?"

"Naw," he said. "Haven't you heard?"

"Heard what?" I asked.

"Hell, I'm leavin' the Senate. Governor Clinton has called a press conference for three o'clock this afternoon to announce that I'm his choice to be the new banking commissioner. I'm leavin' the Senate."

I was floored, of course, but I knew what Jack was telling me could not come to pass.

"You can't do that," I told him.

"Do what?" he asked.

"Jack, I hate to break the news to you, but you can't resign from the Senate to take another state position. I believe it's article 5, in the constitution."

"You gotta be shittin' me," he said.

"I can't believe Bill Clinton and his people don't know this," I cautioned.

"Goddammit, we better see about this."

He wheeled around and left, only to come back in about an hour. He looked at me in disbelief and recounted what had happened. "You were right, Scoop. I can't do that."

"I know, Jack," I said. "Frank White tried to pull the same thing when he was governor when he said he was appointing Lacy Landers from the House as his new labor commissioner."

Later in the day, the governor announced Marlin Jackson as his new choice for the banking position. Jack stayed on with us at the Senate.

The rest of the story is just as amusing. According to Sam Bratton, a Clinton aide, the governor's staff went into hurry-up mode after they found out they couldn't appoint Jack Gibson. Bratton said the staff were sitting around, scratching their heads about a possible selection, when someone said, "Hell, it would take someone with one eye and half sense to even want to be bank commissioner." That's when all the staff members jumped to their feet and, in unison, shouted, "Marlin Jackson!" I'm not sure the story is true, but Sam Bratton said it was. Jackson was a skilled Harvard educated banker and turned out to be a very good bank commissioner.

A second favorite Jack Gibson story is the one about a trip to Dallas. Jack and I were in Big D to watch some Hog basketball when we attempted to rendezvous with some fellow Arkies at a favorite nightspot. We started in when the man at the front door advised us that we both had to have a coat and tie and that Jack could not enter since he was not wearing a tie.

Fine. I instructed Jack, we'd just go to another place. We walked back to the car, and I started to get in when Jack stopped me. "Hold on, Scoop, this ain't my first night out on the town."

I watched in amazement as Jack took off his shoes, removed his two black socks, tied them together, placed them around his shirt collar and drew the knot tight on his new makeshift tie. He straightened his collar, put his blue sport coat back on, and we waltzed right back into the place that had been off-limits just five minutes earlier.

Old age didn't affect Jack's athletic prowess a great deal. He was a very competitive golfer, and he loved coming to my house for the tournament in Sheridan, where I served as tournament director. One year, Jack was partnered with U.S. senator David Pryor. Dozens of state legislators and dignitaries were competing, and a lot of my legislative bosses were staying with me at my house.

Jack started his two days of golf in dramatic fashion by making a hole in one on a 155-yard par 3. His partner, David Pryor, remembers it as "one of my greatest experiences" and tells how Jack removed his new Big Bertha driver from his golf bag, struck the golf ball, and then watched the ball roll the entire 155 yards before plopping into the hole. "Jack was one of the very best people to be with," Pryor would say years later.

Not only did Jack score an ace with the shot that day, but he also won a new $4,000 golf cart as a prize. His luck continued into the next week when we played in Representative Bobby Newman's tournament at Smackover, where Jack won the top door prize—a $3,000 hot tub. The very next week, he entered the Red Apple Inn golf tournament at Heber Springs and won a new set of golf clubs—a pretty good haul over a three-week period.

But the thing I remember most about him staying with me at my home in Sheridan was the tasty treat in the refrigerator that proved irresistible. I was sleeping in my sunroom, and Jack was bedded down on my couch in the adjacent living room. The kitchen was nearby too, and every time I would start to doze off, I would see the kitchen light come on. I had ordered some food for my guests, and the best part of the order was a giant tub of homemade banana pudding. We had eaten some of the tasty dessert before going to bed, but Jack found the pudding irresistible, and he could not go to sleep. I walked into the kitchen and found him bent over the large tub of pudding, holding a giant spoon. He looked up at me and smiled, trying to gulp down another big bite. "Dammit, Scoop, every time I try to shut my eyes and go to sleep, I think about this damn puddin', and I just gotta have more," he said in his high-pitched voice. "I can't stop eatin' this crap."

I understood the urge, reached into the nearby drawer for my own spoon, and joined him. "If we don't finish this off, I'll never get any sleep," he said. So we finished it off, went to bed, and turned out all the lights.

Finally, the most famous Jack Gibson story of all. Part of my job as Senate chief of staff was rounding up the preacher each day to offer up the opening prayer to start the daily business session on the Senate floor. Well, on this day, I was standing on the Senate floor, and the one o'clock starting time was fast approaching when we were still looking around for a minister.

Finally, Max Howell walked over to me and asked about the preacher. "Senator Gibson's man is our preacher today, but I don't know where Jack is," I told Howell.

"Well, you better do something. We need to get started," he growled back.

I looked over to Senator Lu Hardin and asked him if he would fill in and offer our prayer. Howell went to the microphone and started in with his announcement, "Senator Lu Hardin will offer our prayer . . ."

Before Howell could say another word, however, Jack burst through the front door and, in his best bell-ringing voice, declared, "Hold on, Max, I got the goddamn preacher right here."

The room erupted in laughter; even people in the balconies were rolling in the aisles. It was vintage Jack Gibson.

Paul Benham was a big, burly senator from Marianna, a throwback to the plantation-era farming days, a *Gone with the Wind* type of character who talked a lot like Foghorn Leghorn, the cartoon character. He was a likable man, although he suffered occasionally from foot-in-the-mouth disease, which caused him a lot of grief in the press and among legislative colleagues. He pretty much said what was on his mind, no mouth filter as it were, and this often proved embarrassing.

One of my fondest memories of the late senator is a phone call I made to him in 1987. To background this, I would begin by explaining that Wayne Hampton was an old-guard politician from Arkansas County and a friend of mine. He was a state representative and one of the people responsible for hiring me at the legislature. Wayne was also a farmer, and one of his principal crops was rice. Occasionally, he would bring me packets of rice, and some of it was marketed under the name DellaRice, which was a very tasty, sweet blend. After Wayne died, my source for DellaRice dried up. I had talked with Benham one day about his farming operation and decided to give him a phone call to see if he might have some DellaRice.

This was about a week after the Gary Hart incident blew up. Gary Hart was a US senator from Colorado who had announced his candidacy for president of the United States. However, a sex scandal hit the papers that involved Hart and a twenty-nine-year-old model named Donna Rice. Her name, you see, a whole lot like the rice product DellaRice.

So Donna Rice seemed to be a hot topic of conversation at that time I placed my call to the politically astute Benham.

He answered my call, and we chitchatted a few minutes about various things, and then I sensed it was time for me to ask my important question.

"Say, Paul, one reason I called is I wanted to know something— did you ever eat DellaRice?"

Immediately, he answered, apparently still thinking about the sex scandal, which was on everyone's mind at the time.

"Did I ever eat DellaRice? Hell, I never even heard of her," he said.

I dropped my phone on the desk. All Benham could hear on his end of the line was me laughing. And I'm not sure just how long I did laugh.

Another favorite Benham story involves my friend Colleen Cousineau of Atlanta, longtime director of the Southern Legislative Conference organization. Colleen had served as assistant director, and the top job was opening up because of a resignation. She phoned me and asked if I could talk with Benham on her behalf. She was applying for the top spot, and Benham was a member of the SLC's executive committee group, whose members would vote on the new selection. I assured Colleen I would chat with Benham, and later in the day, I found him sitting at his desk in the Senate chamber. I explained about the SLC job opening, and I then made the pitch on behalf of my friend, Colleen.

"Hell yes," Benham promptly answered, "Colleen's been doing most of the work all these years when other people got the credit, and besides all of that, she's got some beautiful tits."

I phoned my friend in Atlanta and told her I had made my pitch with Benham, that he was very receptive, that he liked her hard work, and that he was most appreciative of her tight-fitting dresses, especially the ones with the revealing tops. And yes, Colleen got the promotion.

Benham served a one-year term as Senate pro tem in 1986, filling out the unexpired term of Senator John Bearden, who died in office. During his term, Benham landed on the front page of the newspaper over what was described as the Boogaloo Bill incident. Benham and some others joined then US representative Bill Alexander of Arkansas on a foreign country junket. In front of the press, Alexander shouted "boogaloo" during a performance by an African dance troupe. The comment went viral and hurt Alexander in his reelection effort. Benham, who was present during the incident, was quoted in the media and got his own share of bad publicity.

Soon after the incident, Benham walked into my office to chat. He said he was in Little Rock to attend a highway department meeting, and he asked me to look out my window at a new sign he had put up in his parking space at the capitol. The highway department had made the sign for him, he said, and he was excited about it. It said, "Don't even think of parking here." He had put the sign next to his reserved pro tem parking spot in front of the capitol, not far from where members of the state capitol press corps parked.

I was shocked when he showed me what he had done. "What are you thinking?" I asked the senator.

"You don't like it?" he asked.

"Hey, Chief," I said. "You are all over the newspaper with this Bill Alexander 'boogaloo' stuff, and you put up a sign like that for the press to see?"

"Bad idea, I guess," he answered.

"I'll be right back," I said.

"Where are you going?" Benham asked.

"I'm going to get a sledgehammer and take that sign down before anyone else sees it," I said.

"Oh, I'll do it," he said.

"No, you stay right here. If someone sees you out there with a hammer, they'll think you're putting it up instead of taking it down. I'll be right back."

Benham watched from my window as I removed the offensive sign and placed it in the back of his pickup. The "boogaloo" publicity soon abated, although the incident hurt Alexander in his subsequent attempt to hold on to his office.

Jonathan Fitch of Hindsville was a state senator and a very close friend. I joined with Governor Beebe and others onstage at Old Main in Fayetteville to participate in Jon's eulogy. I had no finer friend, and his death left a huge void in my life. He was a very good legislator, a man who had some ups and downs in his personal life, but none of the senators I knew loved practical jokes any more than my big buddy with the high, squeaky voice did.

Winston Bryant served our state as a legislator, attorney general, and lieutenant governor. As lieutenant governor, he presided over the Senate and did an admirable job as long as he followed Knox Nelson's stern orders and stuck to the script.

But Winston never could get Jon Fitch's name right, and when he would call on the senator to speak, he would usually say, "You're recognized, Representative Finch." This was because Fitch had been a state representative before moving to the Senate, and for some strange reason, Bryant never could get the title or the name right.

And neither could Max Howell. Howell cornered me one day on the Senate floor and said I needed to talk to my friend Fitch about his constant staring. I didn't understand what Howell meant, and I asked him to explain further. "Your friend, Ron Finch, he keeps staring at me like he wants to fight me or something."

I knew he was talking about Fitch, but I did not know until then that Howell was having trouble with Fitch's name too. Fitch had gained a reputation as a man with a wicked temper, and I honestly think Howell was afraid of him.

So the growing problem with the name naturally opened the door for Fitch's buddy pals to affectionately dub him Representative Ron Finch. This moniker stuck with him throughout his days in the Senate and even beyond. In fact, we still call him by that name, even after his passing.

We were headed to Hot Springs, all the Young Golfers, for the Arkansas State University golf tournament. This was a three-day outing at Belvedere Country Club, and we loved the event, which drew a huge crowd of legislators, lobbyists, and ASU alumni.

It had been a while since I had played one of my practical jokes on Fitch, so I deemed the upcoming golf tournament a perfect time to get back into form. Knowing he and his wife planned to stay at the Ramada Inn, I got busy with my plan. I phoned the hotel and asked for the manager, and she promptly got on the phone with me.

"I'm phoning, ma'am, to let you know your hotel will have a special important guest this weekend," I explained to the woman.

"Oh, who is that?" she asked politely.

"Representative Ron Finch and his wife are arriving for the big golf tournament and plan to stay with you," I continued.

"Oh, that's wonderful."

"Yes, ma'am, what I was calling about, I was wondering if you or perhaps someone with the local chamber of commerce—but probably you and your staff—well, if you could welcome him with a greeting on your large sign outside the front entrance?"

She never hesitated. "We would be glad to take care of that. Can you spell his name for me, please."

"Yes. It's Representative Ron Finch," I said as I followed with the letter-by-letter spelling of the name.

I left Little Rock early that Friday and got to the Ramada Inn early. It was beautiful, this huge sign, and the welcome was letter-perfect. I had my camera, so I took a photo and departed for the golf course.

Later that evening, Fitch walked up to me at the cocktail reception.

"Real cute," he started, breaking into his patented grin.

"What?" I asked.

"The damn sign at the hotel. That was real cute."

We broke down and started laughing, and then he told me the rest of the story. It turned out that Fitch and his wife were steering their big Chevy Suburban into the hotel parking lot when they noticed the warm greeting on the sign. Fitch started laughing so hard that he lost control of the vehicle and crashed it into the concrete barrier.

"I'm sorry, man," I said.

"Oh, it was worth it to see that sign," he said. "It didn't hurt my truck much."

Another favorite story involves Fitch and a day on the golf course. Fitch was a big, strong man, tremendously strong and a former football player. But his drink preference was what I called "little girlie drinks," the pink combinations that included a little umbrella swirl stick. He would order them whenever he found a willing bartender who was obliging.

This day, we were sweltering under the summer heat as we made the turn in our golf outing at the Country Club of Little Rock. This meant we were halfway through our round of eighteen holes, and this meant we usually made a quick stop inside the pro shop for a snack of some kind.

The bartender then was a big, rough-looking black man named Robert. I was told Robert had been the bartender there for many years. His demeanor reminded me of the Soup Nazi character on *Seinfeld*, which meant you stepped up to Robert's bar, placed your order in an orderly fashion, stepped to the side, and waited for him to perform his magic.

I did this, ordering a Miller Lite beer and a Snickers bar.

"Anything else?" Robert asked professionally.

"No, sir," I replied.

The rest of our group stepped up and placed their order, and we watched as Fitch strolled in and stepped into Robert's line of fire. Fitch tapped his fingers on the bar, a bit of a drumroll, and finally said, "Uh, give me a fuzzy navel."

I nearly spit out my candy bar. "Jon," I said, "Robert, he won't . . ."

"Won't what?" Fitch asks.

Not missing a beat and looking dead into Fitch's eye, the big, surly barkeep says in a deft monotone, "I don't do no fuzzy navels."

"What?" Fitch asked back.

"I don't do no fuzzy navels!" he repeated, this time with gusto.

"Uh, he'll take a Coke and a bag of chips," I intervened in a snappy voice. "He'll take a Coke and a bag of chips."

Robert pushed the Coke and chips at Fitch, and I ushered him out, as quickly as I could.

"Good lord, Jon, a fuzzy navel?" I asked him as we got outside.

"Well, that's what I wanted." He laughed.

Vic Snyder of Little Rock quickly became a Mike Beebe disciple and a very progressive legislator. But good government and battling Nick Wilson were not on his mind one afternoon when he came to visit. He was concerned about the men's public restroom next to the Senate entrance. He said the small restroom was a busy place and that men standing at the urinal had no privacy because the urinal was next to the front door. Men standing there were "exposed" to the public when the door swung open, and he wanted to know if I could do something about this.

I asked him what he had in mind.

"Maybe have the secretary of state [carpenters] put up some kind of partition so that we're screened off when the door swings open," the senator suggested.

I thought it was a reasonable request, so I went to big boss Max Howell. I told him what Snyder and I had discussed, and the senior senator was ready with his question.

"So how big a project are we talking about here? How big a privacy partition does he want?" Howell asked.

So on top of all the other problems I was dealing with this day, I had to plan the Senate's new bathroom partition. I thought for a minute and answered.

"Senator Howell, I think we're talking about a partition for the senators and other men using the urinal to stand behind while they pee, a sheet of plywood, so just guessing, I'd say a sheet about six inches wide ought to do it."

Howell laughed out loud and then spoke. "Yeah, I think six inches ought to cover everybody out here."

It was one of the few times that Howell and I enjoyed a laugh together. I had the carpentry work done the next day. Senator Snyder was happy, and from then on, he and the others peed in privacy.

One of my busiest times was preparing for the pro tem dinner at the close of the legislative session. In the Senate, this meant a black-tie affair, very fancy and very expensive. Before the ethics law kicked in, this meant hitting up lobbyists to pay for everything, and this was one of my assignments.

I usually turned the fund-raising over to Ron Russell, head of the state Chamber of Commerce. We would go over a list of lobbyists who we thought would want to be involved, and this varied from pro tem to pro tem because each of the pro tems had a favorite lobbyist or two that they wanted involved in the project. The price tag varied according to the pro tem's palate and the gifts involved. Each pro tem handed out gifts to each of his thirty-four colleagues and a few staff. Gifts ranged from expensive crystal to leather travel bags.

After the ethics laws were improved, these dinners were scaled back, and some pro tems changed the way the dinners were financed. Jay Bradford and Mike Beebe had senators contribute $100 apiece to pay for the food and drinks, and Beebe personally paid for the gifts he handed out.

We also changed the way we financed some of the freshman orientation sessions, which had been paid for by the lobbyists before my arrival at the Senate. But the change did not sit well with some members, including Senator Nick Wilson, who liked things first-class. During one freshman dinner at the Capital Hotel, Wilson arrived early, and he and I went over dinner plans and how the bar would be set up. He asked if the two of us had time for a drink before the new senators started to arrive, and I said, "Sure." He looked over the bar supplies and asked, "Is this the best we can do?" apparently not pleased with the hotel's whisky selections.

"It's all my budget can afford, and it's what the hotel picked out under the contract I had to sign," I told Wilson.

Not to be outdone, Wilson picked up a nearby phone, and in a matter of minutes, the best grade of whisky arrived. "I'll pay for this myself," he said with a grin.

"Thank you," I told him as I sipped on my Absolut Vodka martini.

I spent a lot of my time traveling, both in and out of state. There were dinners, roasts-and-toasts, speeches, and filling in when my bosses couldn't fulfill commitments—a lot of nights on the road and a lot of airports and lost luggage. Another part of the job was hanging out with my bosses after the legislature adjourned for the day. Usually, this amounted to Beebe's group heading to a favorite watering hole in Little Rock, having a drink or two, and then winding down with a quiet dinner, usually hosted by a lobbyist, the dinner-arranging chore also a part of my job.

One afternoon, we all gathered around a favorite table at the Afterthought in Little Rock. Beebe, Harriman, and Fitch were giving Hoofman a terse dress-down about his propensity for long speeches. The effusive Hoofman had passed a bill earlier in the day, and his colleagues were trying to explain to him that his long speeches were not really necessary when he already knew the bill was assured of passage.

It was good-natured kidding, and Hoofman was taking the criticism in stride although he was looking desperately for some help when he turned to me for possible support. I had known Cliff for years, our time together going back to earlier days in the House of Representatives when he was a member there and I was an employee. With his Senate friends taking a break from the criticism bombardment, he turned to me, hoping I would take his side.

"Hey," he began with me, "you've heard what our friends here are saying to me, and taking into account that you've known me a long time too, from our days over in the House and so forth, what do you think of what they've had to say, that perhaps I talk too long in some of the speeches?"

His question pretty much proved their point about talking too much, but I paused, took a sip of my martini, and decided I've give it a go. "Cliff," I began, "all I'll say about this is that if I were a death row inmate at Cummins Prison, and they were about to stick the needle in me, and the warden said to me that I had one last phone call, I'd make sure it was to you because if you get on the phone with me, I figure I got at least five or six more hours to live."

The place erupted in laughter, and Hoofman, stung again, dropped his head to the table, knowing that everyone had made their salable point. We've laughed about this several times over the years, and to Cliff's credit, he's a lot more mellow and toned down in his old age. Maybe Beebe appointing him to a judgeship made him less talkative and a better listener.

Two stories, okay three, about Bill Gwatney, and one of them involves Hoofman. As I have said, I admired Gwatzilla so much, and two endearing qualities were his quick wit and unbelievable honesty in expressing his feelings.

A bill had sailed through the House and was making its way to the Senate. It required all persons operating a boat to outfit themselves with a lanyard switch device. Simply put, this is a cord-type string that attaches to one's belt and then to the switch of the outboard motor. In case the operator is thrown from the boat, the motor will automatically shut off. Many operators use these devices, especially on bigger boats such as deep-sea rigs. I read this bill, and I thought it might pose an inconvenience for people such as duck guides and fishing guides who had enough to deal with without having to hook themselves up to an outboard motor. I expressed this concern to Gwatney, who concurred and said he would look at the bill when it arrived at the Senate. He did just that, and he killed the bill, sending it to the trash heap. The bill's sponsor, a sweet old lady from North Arkansas who had never authored a bill before, in the midst of her freshman year in the House, showed up at the Senate and asked to see Gwatney. I pointed him out in the Senate chamber, and she and I walked briskly toward him. She introduced herself to Gwatney and said, "Senator, I want to know why you killed my bill."

True to form and never one to mince words, Gwatzilla smiled and answered, "It was a shitty bill."

My second story about Gwatney centers on an unfortunate episode involving Hoofman. This was a time in our lives when all of us in the Beebe group enjoyed a cocktail or two after work, and Hoofman enjoyed them along with us from time to time. This was long before Hoofman stopped drinking, turned over a new and impressive leaf, and turned away from alcohol.

Hoofman was not a golfer, and he was not with us as we gathered at a golf resort in North Arkansas. We were finishing our day on the links and were drifting in to the condo shared by Beebe and Don Tilton, who were already settled in. I walked in and saw that my friends were huddled around the TV, sitting quietly. I asked, "What's going on?" Beebe quickly hushed me and said, "It's Cliff—he's had a wreck."

The TV news bulletin was reporting that Hoofman had crashed his Chevy pickup at his cattle ranch near Conway and that authorities suspected alcohol might be a contributing factor. One by one, we observed the pictures on the screen, the farm, the scene of the accident, and the beat-up Chevy pickup that showed damage to the front right fender.

And one by one, we began to share our concerns. "Man, this could be bad," Beebe said quietly.

"I just hope he wasn't hurt," I observed.

"I guess we need to try and get a phone call through to him," Tilton suggested.

Then Gwatney, the consummate Chevrolet dealer from Jacksonville who was observing the wrecked pickup on the TV screen, piped up, "Man, it looks like two to three thousand dollars' damage to the right side of that truck."

Typical Gwatzilla, thinking about his next dollar while attempting to allay our fear and concern.

And the third story about my little buddy occurred when Bob Johnson of Bigelow was serving as speaker of the House. A debate had heated up over how the legislature would spend a large amount of surplus money. Johnson and the House members wanted one thing, and Beebe-led forces favored a different plan. None of Beebe's group thought much of Johnson, and a lot of people at the capitol were saying Johnson had let the speaker's job go to his head. During the height of the debate, Gwatney told me and some of his Senate colleagues that he had been handed a note from a state trooper, a note that the trooper told Gwatney had been sent over to the Senate from Johnson. Gwatney showed us the note and said it was a message from Johnson, asking Gwatney to walk over to the speaker's office for a meeting. Beebe asked Gwatney what he thought about the speaker sending a state trooper errand boy with a note to go see him. Obviously not impressed at all, Gwatney pursed his lips and exhaled a puff of air to make a *pfff* noise. Everyone in the room laughed as Gwatney wadded up the note and tossed it in the wastebasket. And to no one's surprise, a few days later, the legislature approved Beebe's plan and not Johnson's plan to spend the money.

The poor state trooper who had been asked to deliver the note worked several legislative sessions for various speakers. And he had to deal with me one day after what the speaker at that time, Bobby Hogue of Jonesboro, described as "an unfortunate misunderstanding."

It happened when Beebe rushed into my office and asked me to get an urgent message to Speaker Hogue about a bill that was pending in the Senate. I said "Sure" because I didn't mind such errands, and Hogue and I had been close friends for a long time.

I left my office and headed for the House. I rarely had time to go to the House, but this was a serious situation, and my message to the speaker was urgent, to say the least.

But unbeknownst to me, the House had implemented a very strict policy concerning visitors, and anyone entering the House chamber had to have an employee badge or certain identifying papers. I had only worked at the capitol twenty or so years, and I didn't have time for such nonsense, and besides, Massanelli and I were well-worn fixtures around both chambers and were asked to travel back and forth to see each many times. But on this day, I was stopped by a new House sergeant and told rather abruptly that I could not enter the side door. I attempted to explain the situation but was told if I wanted to see the speaker, I could fill out new paperwork and wait my turn.

I walked away, refusing to let it bother me, and I knew the sergeant was only doing what he was told. Behind me, I could hear a woman calling out to me, pleading for me to go back. It was the wife of one of the House members, who realized that the sergeant had just screwed up royally, but I kept walking and returned to my office.

A few minutes later, Beebe rushed back in and asked, "What did Hogue say?"

"I don't know," I answered.

"What do you mean, you don't know?" the senator said.

"I didn't get to see Bobby Hogue because the sergeant at arms won't let people from the Senate through the door."

Beebe stormed out of the office, and I returned to my work, not thinking any more about it.

Then a knock on my door. It was Harold Steelman, one of the Senate sergeants who worked for me.

"Bill," Steelman began, "there's a Trooper Donham out here to see you. He says Speaker Hogue sent him."

"Who is it?" I asked

"Trooper David Donham—he says the speaker sent him to see you."

"Tell you what, Coach," I said to Steelman, calling him by the name I first called him when he recruited me to play college ball for him, "have him sign this legal pad, put his name on there and what his business is about, and have him wait outside." I pitched Steelman a yellow legal pad, and he walked away.

About an hour later, Steelman walked back in. "Uh, the trooper is still sitting out here. Do you want him to wait a while longer?"

"Yeah, I'll get to it when I can," I said.

Much later, I asked Steelman to tell the trooper I would not be able to see him and that the lawman could return to his apple-polishing duties in the speaker's office. A few minutes later, my phone rang, and it was Hogue.

"Hey, Scoop, I hear we screwed up," Hogue began.

"Good lord, Hogue-a-boom," I said, calling him by the nickname I always used for him. "Are y'all running some kind of Gestapo over there now?"

"Hey, some of our new people are a little overzealous," the speaker said. "It was an unfortunate misunderstanding, the sergeant has been talked to, and it won't happen again, I promise."

Another big part of my socializing in Little Rock involved what I termed YD. This acronym was my creation for Yates Duty. Joe Yates was a very popular Republican senator from Northwest Arkansas, and when he rolled into Little Rock and "hooked up" with me, I knew I was in for a long evening on the town.

Yates served admirably until term limits sent him home. He was a slow-talking, calculating, shrewd legislator who understood the vagaries of politics, and he fooled a lot of people into thinking he was just an ordinary old country bumpkin who spoke like a hillbilly. But he was a highly educated, brilliant man who could discuss any subject at length while becoming as convincing as any politician in the land. He often shared drinks with Hugh Patterson, the old *Gazette* publisher, at the Afterthought, and there weren't two men more polar opposite than the ultraconservative Yates and the liberal newspaperman who defined aloofness.

But Yates Duty could be an exasperating call to duty because Joe Yates put in long hours once the sun began to set. I was with him at the Afterthought one evening, and we were sharing time with two other friends when Joe Quinn, the channel 11 anchorman, and two other reporters walked through the front door. Quinn waved to me and started toward our table when I turned and tripped over Yates's chair next to me. My action caused Yates to slip from his chair and fall to the floor, and I looked in amazement as he rolled under the table. Hoping that no one saw him, I jumped to my feet and quickly ushered the reporters away into a corner to pretend I needed to talk with them. The senator got to his feet, sat back down, and calmly resumed his conversation with the other guests. I had successfully staved off a possible public relations debacle and an embarrassing lead story on the nightly news.

Another time, Yates and I were at the same bar and had taken pen and paper in with us to relax and work on a roast-and-toast, scheduled for the next day. The event was set to honor Yates, and he was very nervous about all the planning, and I was assisting him with his remarks, jotting down ideas in the dimly lit room as we sipped favorite cocktails.

This went on for several hours, and it was obvious we had overstayed our welcome as our notes became harder and harder to read. I finally told Joe I'd had enough of the work and that I needed to get on home. I left the table briefly to visit the men's room in the rear of the bar. When I returned, Joe was nowhere to be seen. I asked my friend Ray Tucker, who had joined us, about Joe, and he said he thought Joe had left. Ray offered to give me a ride back to the apartment where I planned to spend the night, an apartment at the Capitol Hill building, next to the Capitol. This was also where Yates had an apartment, one floor below where I planned to spend the evening.

I went to bed and rose early the next morning. I phoned my secretary and asked if she wanted me to stop by the donut shop for her on my way in. She said no, and then she asked, "How's Joe?"

"Joe?" I asked. "You mean Senator Yates?"

"Yeah," she said. "Is he going to be all right?"

"What do you mean?" I asked, starting to get concerned.

"The wreck," she said. "The TV said this morning that he wrecked his car last night and was pretty banged up."

I dropped the phone and raced down the stairs in the building to reach Yates's apartment door. After knocking, the door opened slowly, and Yates appeared with a washcloth on his head.

"Oh, hi, Scoop," he drawled.

"Joe, what in the world happened?" I asked.

"Oh, a little fender bender," he said, managing a weak smile.

It turned out that Yates had not left the Afterthought when I was busy in the bathroom and that he drove back after Tucker had given me a ride. A block from the turn-in at the apartment building, Yates's car swerved, and he crashed into a power pole. He suffered head wounds and some severe scratches. His new car was pretty well demolished. That night, we applied a lot of women's makeup to his scratched-up head and face and went ahead with the roast, even though Yates was being featured on all the TV news moments before our program got underway. He took it all in stride, just as he did everything else. He was a ton of fun to be with and one of my all-time favorite friends. And I figure Ray Tucker giving me a ride that night might have saved my life because the car, well, it wasn't much to look at on the TV news clips.

The first time I met Joe Yates was at a duck lodge near Stuttgart. It was a fancy place, owned by Witt Stephens, and Mr. Witt's investment firm regularly hosted groups at the place. This visit occurred while I was still working at the House of Representatives, and our host for the two-day outing was Preston Bynum, who had left the House to work as a lobbyist for the Stephens firm.

Yates and Bynum had been friends since childhood, and Yates was thrilled to be among the group of House members invited to the cabin. It was memorable because it was the first time I had seen a giant-screen TV hooked to a satellite dish. The TV covered one entire wall of the lodge, and the satellite dish outside was as big as a Volkswagen automobile. The only problem was that you had to manually turn the dish in order to receive different channels on the giant TV screen inside.

After dinner and several card games, several of us settled in to watch a pro football game on the giant screen. Bynum asked me to go outside and turn the rusty crank on the dish in order to clear up the TV signal, which was snowy. As I turned, the crank stuck and made a loud popping sound, like it had stripped a gear. Bynum began screaming inside the lodge, "Turn it, Scoop. Keep turning it, Scoop."

I raced in, thinking something was tragically wrong. To my surprise, on the big screen was the most graphic porn movie I had ever seen. A man and woman were in bed and doing all sorts of things. The man was screaming, the woman was screaming, and eight of my House of Representative bosses were staring in disbelief at what was depicted in living color.

John Miller, the saintly speaker, stood in amazement. "My lord," he exclaimed. "I've never seen anything like that in my life."

It was like time was standing still, and Bynum and I were dumbfounded. I couldn't move, and he just stood and stared at me, wondering what in the world had happened.

Finally, my feet began to move, and I ran back outside, trying again to move the crank, but to no avail. It was hopelessly stuck, and the porn show was continuing inside.

I raced back in, and the men were still standing, gasping, and not saying a word—John Miller and Ode Maddox, the elder statesman from Oden; Ernest Cunningham of Helena and Dave Roberts of North Little Rock; Lacy Landers of Benton and Doc Bryan of Russellville; and the colorful Yates, who broke the ice by observing, "That ole gal don't look half bad."

Bynum finally figured out how to disconnect the cable, and the screen went black, and the sound faded. We all had a big laugh, and a TV technician arrived soon from Stuttgart to correct the problem.

A little after midnight, with almost everyone in their bed, I sat on the couch with Cunningham and Bynum, watching the final play of the football game.

"Y'all going to bed?" I asked them.

"I guess," Bynum said. "But we're getting up at four, so it seems kinda a waste to go to bed now."

"Y'all just gonna stay up then?" I asked.

"Yeah, might as well," Bynum said.

"Y'all gonna watch the rest of that movie, aren't you?" I laughed.

So we did. The three of us stayed up the rest of the night, eyes glued to the big screen. Yates was right . . . the old gal did look pretty good.

CHAPTER 27

In a later chapter, I'll quote a lobbyist for the trucking industry who told me one day that when a person lobbies the legislature, "money talks and bullshit walks." That said, I feel compelled to write something about what I saw and didn't see and what was said and not said and what I suspected and didn't suspect in the way money impacts the legislative process.

We all know that big money is a huge part of the political process and growing bigger all the time, thanks to the quirky US Supreme Court ruling that greased the way for corporations to give as much as they want with no strings attached.

Money is a big part of government from city hall to the White House, and this includes our state legislatures. When Max Howell and Knox Nelson were in power during my early years at the Senate, everyone knew that they were the men to turn to if you wanted legislation enacted into law. Without their support, a pending bill had absolutely no chance at passage—no chance at all—and lobbyists knew they better be financially supportive of the two giants.

The "cleanest" way for lobbyists to get their bill passed was to find a friendly legislator who had seniority and knew the ropes. A committee chairman was the best person for this task. If a lobbyist wanted to kill legislation, he went about this the same way. He would have the bill drafted, find a friendly legislator who would become the bill's sponsor, and then see to it that the bill quietly went away, getting bogged down as the long legislative session wore on.

For instance, let's say you are the lobbyist for the trucking industry, and a fuss is being made about gravel trucks breaking car windshields. Your industry does not want to require expensive tarps on every truck, so your company hires a lobbyist. The lobbyist gets a lawyer to draft a new bill that will require every gravel truck in Arkansas to install one of the tarps. This proposed bill silences the critics since it appears the legislature is addressing the issue. Your lobbyist goes to a favorite representative, and the bill sails through committee and is voted out of the House. But suddenly it hits a snag in the Senate, and the sponsoring legislator pulls it down during the last week of the session, and the bill dies. The issue fades away, the industry goes on about its business, and the lobbyist picks up his big paycheck, having dutifully killed the legislation. And the representative who has agreed to handle the bill and see to it that it cleverly went away—well, he gets a big, fat campaign check from the industry and probably the lobbyist. If he is dishonest, and the lobbyist is dishonest, the legislator reaps more than a campaign contribution.

The big question in political discussions is whether money is handed under the table. Are politicians bought off? Most people involved in the legislative process at the capitol would only laugh at the question and walk away without revealing their true feelings.

Before his death, a lobbyist from Little Rock took time to sit with me and talk politics one last time. He told me his medical prognosis was not good, and he asked if I still intended to write a book on my days in politics. He agreed to talk about some topics he had considered "off the table" from previous chats over the years, including payments he and a client had made to legislators long before the term limits amendment passed in 1992. I told him I wanted to hear the stories if he felt like talking.

He said he was successful in passing 100 percent of his client's legislation over the years. And he said he had a very "simple formula" in getting the job done. His formula was that he made large cash payments to two veteran legislators, both of whom served in the Senate. He said he also made sure a veteran House member "was taken care of," but not to the tune demanded by the two old pros in the Senate.

He wouldn't give me the names of the three men, but I pressed him to tell me the amount of the payments.

"Oh, I'll tell you." He laughed. "Each of the senators received $20,000 at the start of each legislative session, whether or not I even had a bill for consideration," he explained. "It was just our way of agreeing to do business."

And the House member?

"Well, let's just say he looked at things a little bit different," my friend said. "He liked to be taken care of on trips, and he liked presents for his wife. Nothing real expensive, but it added up over time. He did tell me his wife liked expensive negligees, and she preferred the colors black and red. I didn't buy the clothes—I left that to him."

He also said several House members loved "borrowing" his credit cards from time to time for expensive meals while in Little Rock. "They didn't have any trouble asking, and they sure didn't have any trouble buying the meals for themselves and their friends, lots of friends sometimes."

He said he wasn't sure how many, if any, other lobbyists offered up cash payments in this manner. "We could have all gone to jail, and I knew that then, just like I know it now," my friend said. "It's not something I'm proud of now, now that I look back on it, but I had a job to do, and they were very willing participants. I'm just glad I didn't get caught. I figured the two payments were a cheap way of making sure my business was taken care of. I didn't have to do a whole lot of other spending."

He said he had several unusual requests for financial help from legislators, but two he would always remember were from House members.

"One House member wanted me to pay for the big orchestra at his daughter's wedding in Little Rock, and another House member, a woman, was always hitting me and other lobbyists up for money to buy her hats. She had a lot of pretty hats, expensive hats."

He said the $20,000 cash payments to the two senators were made in $5,000 installments. He said he paid the men in their private offices, adjacent to the Senate chamber. "I felt pretty greasy after I gave it to them," he said. "I felt like I needed to go home and take a bath. But I did it over a ten-year period, and I got done what my bosses wanted done."

A friend from Northeast Arkansas told me the story of visiting with a very powerful Central Arkansas senator prior to a legislative session in the 1990s. Oil company executives wanted a bill passed in the upcoming session, and my friend was assigned the task of meeting with the influential senator at his office in Little Rock. He said he went there with $10,000 in cash in his briefcase, ready to complete the assignment. But he said he became so infuriated over the senator's arrogance he walked out of the meeting and never opened his briefcase.

"The longer I sat there, the more I hated the arrogant son of a bitch," my friend said, never flinching over his assignment to pay the man $10,000, no questions asked.

The only time I witnessed a questionable situation involving money was when I walked into Knox Nelson's office unannounced. He was standing behind his desk and handing hundred-dollar bills to three House colleagues. It may well have been a very innocent transaction or maybe even a poker bet, but I always suspected I had walked in on something that took them by surprise, not to mention the surprise it caused me. The senator and I never mentioned it in our years of subsequent work together.

Another time, I was out on the town with a well-known lobbyist who was venting about a senator who, the lobbyist said, had "double-crossed" him and his company by changing his vote on a bill. The bill had been debated for several weeks in the Public Health, Welfare, and Labor Committee, and everyone knew the question of its passage would come down to a razor-thin vote.

The lobbyist was angry because the senator had told him he would vote no and help kill the bill, which was what the lobbyist wanted. But when the final vote came up, the senator switched and voted for the bill and against what the lobbyist had been told.

After several strong drinks, the lobbyist opened up about how he had lobbied the senator. "I paid the guy's filing fee, I funded his entire reelection campaign, I buy his suits and silk ties at the finest men's store in Little Rock, I pay for his wife's shopping trips to Dallas, fly her down there, and pay for all of her clothes, and then he stabs me in the back," the lobbyist fumed. He said he would never trust the senator again, nor would his company.

The lobbyist's employer was one of the state's biggest insurance companies, and I was allowing him to talk as much as he wanted, and he continued on as more drinks were served. He said he and his company had supported the senator for years and that the senator was their go-to guy at the legislature. "He doesn't have any trouble taking my money, my company's money, and then we find out his word is no good," the lobbyist continued.

At this point, I asked the lobbyist just how deep the relationship went as far as financial arrangements were concerned.

He answered that he would be glad to tell me, adding that his company had made the senator's life "pretty damn nice." He said his company had spent $60,000 on one of the senator's campaigns and that he suspected most of that money went into the senator's "hip pocket." He said he had showered the senator's wife with meals, travel, shopping trips, and even a trip to New York to see Broadway shows. The lobbyist said his wife even accompanied the senator's wife on shopping sprees to Dallas.

He talked on into the night, but he was never specific about how the payments were made to the senator and whether other lawmakers were also on his company's secret payroll.

It was no secret that many of the senators and representatives, who were lawyers, were hired by various companies and placed on yearly retainers. This was legal, but it raised some serious ethical questions from time to time. Also, it was well-known that some businesses did business with nonlawyer legislators, all on the up-and-up legally but certainly questionable in the eyes of some.

Another lobbyist hinted very strongly in a casual conversation with me near the end of my legislative career that certain legislators were provided free automobiles from certain financial interests, but he was never specific. He did say that some legislators were given Lincoln Continental cars by one lobbyist and that another lobbyist had provided a new Cadillac to a legislator. The lobbyist said certain committee chairmen were "never without the necessary funds" needed to make their lives comfortable, but he did not elaborate, and I did not pursue the matter.

I remember Bill Simmons, a reporter for the *Democrat-Gazette*, asking Mike Beebe in my office about whether he thought attempts were being made to buy influence. Beebe assured the reporter that he had never been privy to anything like that but that he was offered cash contributions, legal at that time, when he first announced his intentions to run for the Senate. Beebe said a group of farmers and businessmen met at an Arkansas County residence and that the men had taken up a cash collection to give to him. He said he refused the money and told them if they wanted to contribute to his campaign, they could write checks that would be recorded as official contributions rather than make cash contributions. At the time, Simmons was working on an article about legislators who he said may have accepted walking-around money, or $100 handshakes from lobbyists. But no article ever materialized.

There was occasional talk about payoffs to legislators when big, controversial bills were on the schedule. These might include measures affecting high finance, banking, and insurance.

After one such bill passed the Senate, a young, inexperienced senator from East Arkansas walked into a room, apparently feeling no pain after several cocktails and bragged about his new, shiny Cadillac, a payoff gift, he said, from a high-rolling stock investor who sent the car as a thank-you for the senator's vote. I wasn't sure about the accuracy of the senator's story, but I did take a ride in the new car, and it was a beauty.

The best-known stories were about the so-called walking-around money. This story surfaced at every session, that certain lobbyists gave legislators $100 handshakes as a way of ensuring walking-around money while they were in Little Rock. An administrative assistant to one well-known liquor lobbyist told me that her boss made a practice of $100 walking-around gifts every session and that House members lined up regularly at her boss's office for the secret gifts. "It makes me sick to see them in here," she told me in disgust. She said one young House member from North Arkansas was constantly at her boss's office, seeking the handy cash handouts, which, she said, her boss gladly handed over.

One lobbyist told me the biggest abusers of the political system were some of the county judges, not legislators. The lobbyist sold heavy equipment for a living, and he said it was "a constant fight" over which lobbyist could pay the most under the table for some county judges' business. He said the "going price" for doing business with some judges was $2,000 cash. "If I wanted to sell some of them a piece of expensive equipment, I better be ready to put $2,000 in a few pockets," the lobbyist told me.

The lobbyist said he never made the payments at the judge's office or even in the judge's hometown. "I'd take him to his favorite restaurant in Little Rock, we'd have something to eat, and then I'd give him his money, which we called his 'dessert.'" On one occasion, the lobbyist said, he almost forgot to hand the money over and later gave the judge his money while the two of them were in the restaurant's bathroom.

Today, much has changed. Arkansas has a functioning Ethics Commission, and campaign contributions are now a matter of public record and available on the Internet. A lot of lobbyists are heavy contributors, giving the maximum allowed by law, while others limit their gifts in accordance with new guidelines. One lobbyist told me recently over lunch that he was in Little Rock to hand out checks to legislators. He said many lobbyists, including himself, prefer to wait until legislative races are over and then make their contributions. He said it is still "very costly" to be a lobbyist but not like it was prior to term limits.

"Man, there was a time when one or two senators were taking all of my budget," the lobbyist said with a laugh. "Now, I give out $1,000 checks and try to spread it around as best I can."

The arrest and prosecution of Nick Wilson in 1999 probably put a damper on a lot of careless behavior on the part of everyone involved in the Arkansas political process—at least for a while. And the subsequent conviction of Senator Paul Bookout of Jonesboro and the probe of former senator Gilbert Baker of Conway in an apparent far-reaching investigation into questionable contributions made everyone stand up and take notice. Knowing that the FBI and federal prosecutors are clever enough to infiltrate and put people away can have a chilling effect, for sure.

A lot of people were secretly taped in the long investigation of Wilson, and the recordings were very revealing about how some politicians and bureaucrats can abuse the system with a goal of making money.

One sidebar here to that whole episode involving senators and House members and the secret recordings arranged by gubernatorial aide Neal

Turner who, authorities say, escaped prosecution after he and his wife agreed to cooperate with authorities. As the top aide to the governor, Turner was everywhere at the capitol. He played golf with senators and House members, ate and drank with them, and talked legislative strategy constantly. He became a close friend to many of us, and it came as quite a shock when it was revealed that he was working with federal authorities in bringing a case against legislators, including Wilson.

But it didn't really surprise me, and my friends still laugh at me when I say that Turner was a plant from the beginning. As a reporter, I spent a great deal of my time with undercover agents from various law enforcement agencies, including federal and state agencies. They were some of the most proficient, clever men I had ever seen, the way they could disguise themselves and work their way into crime situations. Nothing surprised me after I watched them for a while. I knew one undercover agent with the Arkansas State Police who busted the same drug dealer three times by using different disguises. He was like the old TV cop Beretta, and the other agents who ran with them were just as clever.

Neal Turner came along in Arkansas politics about the same time the FBI was putting undercover agents into several states to look into suspected criminal dealings inside state legislatures. Some of these undercover agents, as reported on the CBS news show *60 Minutes*, were ex-college football coaches, and this was a job Turner held before moving into politics in Governor Tucker's office.

Turner secretly taped several Arkansas lawmakers during the probe that led to Wilson's downfall. And what punishment did Turner and his wife receive? Well, I think the word *zero* readily comes to mind.

Was he working from the inside all along? My friends still laugh at me when I offer up this theory, but I'm not laughing. I remember how clever those men I worked with were, and I wouldn't put anything past them.

So back to the question of whether I thought senators and representatives took cash payoffs. Clever politicians answer tough questions by repeating the question that was asked of them and then answering. So I'll do that in summing up. Do I think some legislators I knew received money under the table? Yes, I certainly do. Can I prove that in any way? No, I cannot. Do I think it still occurs? Yes, although the parties involved are more clever now, setting up PACs and finding ways around newly enacted ethics laws.

CHAPTER 28

My last day at the capitol passed quickly and quietly. I had some time alone in my spacious, new office to think back over my nineteen years in the Senate and the seven years in the House. I was only thirty-two when I signed on with Speaker-Elect John Miller, and now I was walking away at age fifty-eight, having fulfilled my pledge to pro tem Jim Hill to stay on through the bulk of his tenure as head of the Senate. A new job awaited back home in Sheridan, an opportunity that came my way out of the blue and one I relished. I had already met with my new board of directors and local officials to secretly agree to my new position, and I was thrilled over the opportunity. I was also putting the finishing touches on my novel, *Benchwarmer*, and I was anxious to spend time with my publisher about the new deal I was about to sign. Going into a new job is always exciting, and it was a stimulating feeling I hadn't felt in more than a quarter of a century. Hill and his close ally, Senator Shane Broadway, met with me and asked if I might postpone my departure for six weeks, until they had time to find a replacement, but I politely declined. I had made up my mind, the new job awaited, and being decisive was one of the personal traits I valued, almost above all the rest.

Some of the new senators who were not on Hill's team were ready for me to leave too. Three of them had been stung by a newspaper column that placed them in the "worst" member category, and some anonymous quotes in the article were attributed to a Senate staffer. Some of those listed in the worst category thought I might have been the anonymous source that criticized them, and I chose not to respond to their insidious behavior. My reasoning was simple: I knew what I had said to the reporter, and I also had my own ideas about who had made other comments.

I never divulged then what I knew. One reason was that I really didn't care what any of those on the worst list thought about me or the newspaper. And number 2, the newspaper was entitled to its opinion, and I did not necessarily disagree with any of their selections except the naming of Mahony, my friend, as one of the worst. And thirdly, I knew who actually nominated some for the list, but I didn't think it was my place to tell everyone what I knew at that time.

Years later now, it doesn't faze me to tell what I know about the person I think suggested some nominees. The person was a man who worked privately for Senator Hill, the pro tem. After the newspaper article appeared, I was in Hill's office, and this man and others were present. We were speculating about the article and actually laughing about some of the reporter's observations and who may have said what. Hill and others opened up about how they had talked with the reporter while suggesting nominees, and I told them I had also chatted with the reporter. We agreed that whomever the newspaper considered best and worst was so subjective it mattered very little to senators and insiders who actually made the final list. But as I left the office, Hill's personal employee told me he had not only talked with the reporter, but he had also gone so far as to even give the reporter his penciled-out list of his choices for some awards. It was the man's right to do as he pleased, and I don't know who he actually nominated, but I couldn't comment at that time on what he had told me because I was totally loyal to Hill, my friend and big boss, and the other man was one of his personal aides.

As the controversy grew and some of the "worst" senators became more infused with anger, I refused to comment about the entire brouhaha. One senator was very critical of me, but I really was not concerned because I had my new job lined up, and this critic was not taken seriously by anyone at the capitol. In fact, years earlier, Bud Canada, the old senator from Hot Springs, had described this particular senator as "a top-water choir boy with an ugly mustache." And the man was quickly becoming a frequent target of the press because of his frequent travels at taxpayers' expense. One senator called the traveling senator Junketman and quietly sang the Elton John song "Rocket Man" when he walked into the room.

Jim Holt of Springdale, an ultraconservative Republican, was also on the worst list, and he expressed his dislike for me to reporters. Holt had not liked me for several months prior to the article being published after I had to call him down for misuse of the Senate chamber. It happened when he informed me late one afternoon, as the daily session was winding down, that he had a group of friends from his hometown coming in for a visit and that they might want to tour the Senate chamber later that evening.

I told him a sergeant at arms would be on duty and that the sergeant could watch for the group and show them where to enter the large room. The visit took place, but it was not at all what Holt had said it would be. The sergeant, my head sergeant, in fact, came to see me the next day, upset over what had happened the night before. He said the group arrived at the Senate with Holt leading them, that Holt instructed them to take a seat in the senators' chairs even though this was forbidden, and that a full-fledged revival-style prayer meeting broke out and lasted more than an hour, with Holt leading them not only in prayers and Christian testimony but in election-day strategy discussions as well.

I told the sergeant I would talk with Holt, and I did. I told the new senator the Senate had strict rules on how the chamber was to be used and that political events and campaigning were strictly forbidden. He was offended, and I knew I had made an enemy, someone who would strike back at me first chance. But once again, I didn't care because I knew I was headed home to a new job, and I also knew that I had been criticized by men of unquestionable character, a quality I thought this particular senator was severely lacking.

The incident reminded me of two other events much earlier when I actually did care about hurting people's feelings. The first was when a young Little Rock lawyer-doctor announced his plans to seek a Senate seat against incumbent Doug Brandon, the well-known furniture dealer from Little Rock. The young upstart was named Vic Snyder, who turned out to be a whale of a legislator who went on to a very distinguished career in Congress. But Snyder's premier announcement for the state senate caused me to leave a meeting and rush back to the Senate for some heated discussions.

I paused from my meeting to phone my secretary, and it was a good thing I did. She said all hell had broken loose because Snyder, this political unknown, had waltzed into the Senate, talked with Senate secretary Hal Moody, an old Max Howell disciple, and had announced his candidacy in the Senate Quiet Room.

"He held his press conference in the Senate Quiet Room?" I asked my secretary Eileen.

"Yes," she said, "and Hal let him in and even stayed in there while he talked to the press."

This sent me into orbit. No one, not even the sitting senators, were allowed to use the Senate chamber, Quiet Room, or any of the offices for political purposes. It was probably the most important of all the rules.

I rushed back to the office and tore into Moody, an old man who never stood up to anyone. "Well, he seemed like a real nice man, and I just let all the reporters in," he told me.

Snyder had used the Senate's plush surroundings, the leather chairs, and mahogany tables, to announce against Brandon because Brandon's furniture store had sold the Senate the furniture. He made his point, and it looked bad for Brandon, but Brandon was doing business with many of the state departments, and at that time, his dealings were perfectly legal and not in violation of any law or ethics procedure.

Snyder won his race, and he became a very capable senator, joining with Beebe in helping oust Nick Wilson from power. Brandon, one of the Senate's best tax experts, was crushed by the defeat and died a short time later.

One other incident over the use of the Senate chamber caused me to lose support from a senator, this time an old ally. Jerry Bookout had retired from the Senate even though he returned later, but when this happened, he had given up politics and gone back to his family business in Jonesboro.

It was late in the afternoon, closing time, and Bill Clinton was settling in as the new president in Washington. Arkansas was besieged with reporters still wanting the Arkansas story on Clinton, his early days in politics, and his time at the state capitol. We were used to dealing with the reporters who seemed to be interviewing everyone under the sun who had worked with the man from Hope.

I had left my office to walk into the back rooms of the Senate to ask my employee, William Parks, to start shutting things down for the day. But I noticed the east door into the huge Senate chamber cracked open, and I peered inside. To my surprise, the giant room was filled with bright studio lights and cameras. People were running around everywhere, and one of the people, a film director, was shouting instructions. At the front of the room, Jerry Bookout was posed, going over some notes and in full rehearsal mode.

"What in the world is going on?" I asked in an angry voice.

"Oh, hi, Scoop," Bookout began. "This is a film crew from the BBC, and we're filming a special on Bill Clinton."

I couldn't believe what I was seeing. I turned to the BBC man in charge and waved my hand. "Get out of here, get all your stuff, and these people and get out of here!"

Bookout looked sheepishly at me and started walking. "Hey, did we screw up?" he asked.

"Hey, Chief," I began, calling him by an old, familiar name. "You know we can't do this. If I let you do this for Clinton, then all my Republican senators are gonna jump down my throat."

I found out later that one of my employees had mistakenly given Bookout the "okay" to use the chamber. It was a big misunderstanding, but there wasn't much I could do about the possible damage it had caused. Years later, when Bookout returned as a full-voting senator, I knew he would always remember the film crew incident, and I also knew I would never have his full support again. Once again, I could have taken the path of least resistance, joining with the other staff person in letting the incident slide, but I tried to be fair in the job, and I knew the rules had to be upheld, for Democrats and Republicans, for Jim Holt, a new man, and Bookout, my old ally.

CHAPTER 29

Occasionally, reporters would write about my job at the Senate, especially the social end of it, which involved my work and association with lobbyists and the dozens of organizations in the state that had business with the legislature. But the "social calendar," as we called it, was and still is a huge part of the work that goes on with the Arkansas legislature and every other legislature around the country. Every group and every paid lobbyist want their few precious minutes with the legislature, and this is usually done through a scheduled event, although full-time lobbyists never stray far from the capitol building, even when the legislature is not in session.

I freely admit I spent a great deal of time being wined and dined in my quarter century at the legislature, but I also know how I was raised by a good mother and father, and I can honestly say there was never a corrupting moment in all my political dealings. I traveled extensively, but I never made a secret of what I was doing, and when the new ethics laws kicked in, I made sure my sojourns and any lobbyist-afforded social courtesies were duly reported. I look back on my travels and those good times, and I don't regret any of them. To say I do, well, would be, as Jim Hill always liked to say, "a bit disingenuous." Hill loved that word.

I'll put it my own way, or in Sheridan talk, as Ray Thornton would say, to say I didn't enjoy it—well, I would be lying through my teeth. I know, even today, I treated everybody fairly and equally, and I was committed to doing just as much for a newcomer lobbyist as I was for the men and women who became my friends. Some of the best lobbyists I worked with were employed by the Arkansas Press Association, and they represented some of the very columnists who were occasionally ranting about the way I did my job.

I do know that I played golf on the finest courses, fished for blue marlin off the coast of Mexico, dined at some of the finest restaurants in the world, and sat on the front row in the big arena in Charlotte in 1994 when Nolan's Razorbacks beat Duke for the national championship. I loved it, and I did a lot of those things with lobbyists whose expense accounts helped pay the tab. I relished the opportunities that came my way, and even today, some of those lobbyists who were jetting around the country with me remain my closest buddy pals, and I don't have a clue as to what their political agendas involve. They never asked one out-of-line favor of me during my time at the capitol, and they haven't asked me to do them a favor since. I still golf with a handful of them, and I am proud to call them friends.

I was at the hospital recently when one of them went through cancer surgery. He had sat with me six years earlier at the hospital when I too battled the same frightening disease. It's what friends do, and a line of work—a job description—has absolutely not one thing to do with it. Lobbyists are often branded as special interests, but there are some exceptionally bright, witty, and progressive men and women in the profession who add a lot to the political debate and, more often than not, provide answers to some of the nagging problems we all face.

Yes, some lobbyists do bad things, some are real douche bags, but I think this applies to every profession. In fact, some of those newspaper columnists who wrote about me from time to time never bothered to offer up a "correction" when they were horribly wrong. One even told me he didn't have time to check his facts before his article went to press. And we wonder why journalism has sunk to new lows.

I mentioned earlier about the columnist who reported in his big Sunday space that I was attending a three-day duck hunt in East Arkansas when, in fact, I was a hundred miles away, at home, in church, and serving communion. My minister was so appalled over the inaccurate report that he asked me if it would be okay with me if he telephoned the reporter. I told him not to do it, that the writer was not inclined to print a correction, and that the article didn't faze me one way or the other.

A memorable clash I had with a reporter occurred near the end · of my career at the capitol when the Senate was wrapping up its huge multimillion-dollar renovation. As we finished up, I told my bosses that I wanted to create a new art program so that we could display original paintings rather than put up some kind of cheap, store-bought framed prints. The Senate had enjoyed some beautiful framed works from the Arkansas History Commission, thanks to Senator Nick Wilson, but that project had been discontinued, and I wanted to set up a new program of my own.

I remembered that my sister, Joy Greer, had started a program years earlier at her downtown bank that commissioned Arkansas artists to display their works, and I set out to do the same thing at the Senate. I turned to an old friend, Carolyn Taylor, a well-known Arkansas artist. Carolyn owned a studio in my hometown and had opened a second space at Hot Springs. I phoned her with my idea, and she offered several suggestions for involving Arkansas artists. I asked her to head a committee whose members would select the artists and art. The committee included Taylor and lobbyists Don Tilton and Martha Miller, two ardent art collectors. Even though Tilton was my close friend, it was Taylor who actually suggested we include him because he was a frequent visitor to her studio in Hot Springs, and he had purchased many of her paintings and numerous paintings from other Arkansas artists.

The committee went to work and computerized a list of Arkansas artists. They contacted the artists and compiled a list of those willing to rotate their works in and out of the Senate every six months, free of charge. Dozens of participants joined in, and they ranged from those well-known, like the *Democrat-Gazette*'s John Deering, to those not so well-known, like the wife of one of the senators. The list was quite impressive, and the paintings started to roll in, and they were stunning. Word spread around the capitol and the entire state about my new program, and I was very proud of the way things were shaping up. The secretary of state, Charlie Daniels, even contacted me about expanding the project so that the artists' works could appear throughout the huge capitol building.

But when you deal with the public and the press, you have to be on guard and prepare for the negative feedback, even though I did not in my wildest dreams ever believe a reporter could see anything wrong with this new effort.

But my phone rang, and it was a Little Rock reporter. She asked about the program and the idea behind it, and I went into great detail about the program and how impressive the collection had become. She seemed very positive too, apparently listening carefully and taking notes as we talked. We ended our conversation, but in less than a minute, my phone rang again, and it was the reporter calling back.

"Oh, my editor [she called him by name] wanted me to ask you one other question," she said. "He wants to know how much [money] you're making off all this."

I couldn't believe my ears. What a horrible, leading, insulting accusation. To imply, to insinuate, to bait me into something like that . . . I just sat back for a moment, and then I answered: "So [your boss] asked you to call and ask me that?" I asked.

"Yes," she answered.

"Well, maybe [your boss] is listening on the other line, and that's fine, and I hope he is, so you tell [your boss] not to ever call me again or ask to see me again."

"You're saying . . ." she said.

"You heard me. Now two things—number 1, tell [your boss] that the last artist we signed just this morning to bring art to the Senate is his cousin from Northwest Arkansas, not that he would give a damn, and number 2, I assume, you being a fine, veteran reporter, I assume you can count to five, is that right?"

"You want me to count to five?" she asked.

"Yeah," I said. "Start counting."

"One, two, three . . ."

At three, I slammed the phone down. It was so typical of some of the press, the deplorable way they treat people. Neither the reporter nor her boss cared about the art program or the opportunities it presented—they only wanted to stir up controversy.

I tried to be honest and up-front not only with my bosses but also with the lobbyists and trade representatives. Some of the most effective lobbyists were college presidents, and I got to know several of them through my work and socially. One of my favorite lobbyist stories involved a man named Michael, who lobbied only two years.

Michael was a handsome, well-dressed, outgoing Little Rock businessman. He registered as a lobbyist and was partnered with an old friend of mine from Stuttgart. They were lobbying primarily for agricultural interests, but I was never sure of their entire clientele.

The Arkansas State University golf tournament was scheduled for North Hills Country Club in North Little Rock, and Michael asked me to be his partner for the weekend event. I usually played in the tournament, and it was a time for me to spend quality moments with Mike Beebe and others who also played. The event was becoming very popular with legislators because of the work of Don Tilton, who at that time was employed by the university as a government liaison and legislative lobbyist.

Golfers are treated to a big dinner, and this is a time when wives and significant others arrive in their finery. We had finished our Friday round of golf and had arrived back at the club for cocktails before the dinner. I was standing at the bar with Senator Allen Gordon of Morrilton, Tilton, and my partner Michael, and we were making small talk, mostly about the day's round of golf. Michael, new to the legislative scene, had just introduced himself to Senator Gordon, and the evening was off to a pleasant start as we chatted. Gordon was waiting for his wife, Phyllis, to arrive, but none of us knew this at that time. Phyllis is a tall, beautiful, blue-eyed blonde who has movie-star looks. Michael was the only member of our group who had never met the senator's wife, and he wasn't aware that she would be arriving, either, which set the scene for an impending debacle.

As we sipped on our drinks, Phyllis entered the room through a large glass door in the back of the crowded room. She was *styling* in a sequined long evening grown, and her long blond hair was flowing over her shoulders. I saw her, and I moved toward her husband to alert him that his wife had arrived, but I was interrupted by my new friend, Michael. Standing only a few inches from Allen Gordon and seeing the gorgeous blonde walking into the room, not knowing that she is the senator's wife, Michael blurted out, "Who is that knock-dead gorgeous thing that just walked in?"

In most instances such as this, you could hear the proverbial pin drop, but I could see this potential disaster occurring in freaky slow motion. I seemed to always sense things before they happened, especially if they had the potential for disaster.

I stopped Michael in midsentence, before he could finish describing the senator's wife in more detail.

"Michael, you always do the same old thing at these parties," I began. "You find a senator's wife and pull this same old joke, pretending to fall in love with their wife."

Michael has this puzzled look on his face as I give him a slight nudge, trying to get him to hush.

"You know that's Allen's wife, Phyllis, and your jokes just aren't funny anymore," I continued, seeing this wide-eyed look on Michael's face as he finally starts to realize his impending giant faux pas.

Allen moved away and greeted his wife with a hug. Michael quickly moved me away to an adjacent room and took several deep breaths before speaking. "God, Scoop," he began calling me by my nickname. "You saved me, man. What can I do?"

"Nothing," I advised. "I think you've done enough. Allen didn't notice anything, and besides, he realizes how pretty his wife is. But hey, you need to watch your mouth in this business. One mistake like that, and your lobbying career is over."

"Hey," he said, "anything, anything you ever need from me, just ask. I love you, man."

In all my dealings, I only had one lobbyist who seemed to get angry with me. And it really wasn't with me; he seemed to be angry at the whole legislative process. He worked for the trucking industry, and he was not their lead man, Lane Kidd. But he was walking with Kidd the day he seemed to lose his cool with me. The truckers were involved in an issue that had passed the House and was scheduled for debate in the Senate. Kidd and his minions were working hard on the bill, but they were having a hard time scheduling time with the senators to present their side. The assistant to Kidd stopped me near the front entrance of the Senate and asked me if I could help him meet one of the senators who seemed opposed to their legislation. He explained that the senator seemed to be dodging him, and I told him I would look into the situation and give him a call if he would leave his telephone number. I told him the senator usually had time in the afternoon after the Senate recessed for the day.

"That's just more bullshit," the man fired back, a response that caught me by complete surprise. "He ain't gonna talk with me because he's afraid to talk with me. Out here, you get to see these guys one way—you gotta buy their vote because money talks and bullshit walks."

He stormed off, and I never saw the man again. To this day, I don't know what his problem was, but I know he had some very strong convictions about the legislative process, and I don't think any of his feelings were positive.

I was in Las Vegas for a national legislative meeting, and an Arkansas lobbyist wanted to host a dinner for the Arkansas senators in attendance. I agreed to help him with the event, which we scheduled for Sunday evening, our first night in town. The dinner was arranged, and everyone had a good time.

The lobbyist then arranged the same type of dinner for the Arkansas House members in attendance for the following evening. Later, I asked him how the dinner with the House members turned out, and he told me, "I really don't want to talk about it."

I pursued the matter, and he repeated what he said, adding, "If I tell you what happened, you'll just get mad."

Well, I did pursue further, and he finally gave in. He said he arrived for the dinner fifteen minutes late after his cabdriver got lost in downtown Las Vegas. The Arkansas House members were already at the restaurant when he walked in. He said he was embarrassed to be late for the dinner he had set up, but the situation was out of his control. He said he greeted his guests and told them about his cab ride and that most seemed understanding until he reached two female House members who were standing in the corner of the room, sipping a cocktail. He said he apologized to the two of them about being late and assumed they would be understanding, until one of them spoke. "I'm sure if you had been hosting Mike Beebe and Nick Wilson, you would have been on time," the woman snipped.

I couldn't believe what the lobbyist was telling me. He was right because I became angry when I heard what he had to say.

"Unbelievable," I said. "You're paying for the drinks and dinner, and they're standing there saying stuff like that," I said.

"I told you, you would get mad," he said to me. "That's why I didn't want to tell you what happened."

"You know the difference in what happened?" I asked him, following up with my own answer. "The difference in those two women and the senators is that if you had been fifteen or twenty minutes late to our dinner, we wouldn't have been ready to jump you. We would have been worried about you, worried that something bad had happened to you, and Mike Beebe and Nick Wilson would have bought *you* a drink when you got there rather than you having to buy them a drink."

But he was right; it made me furious. I hated the way some legislators treated the lobbyists, but they had to smile and take it.

I had been in my new job at the Senate for only a month when I saw Max Howell berate a lobbyist. The Legislative Council was convening, and many of the House and Senate members were congregating in a back room where the coffeepot was located. Representative Bobby Newman of Smackover motioned for Carey Baskin, a phone company lobbyist, to go back into the room. Newman said he had an important question for Baskin about a proposal on the committee's agenda.

Howell saw the stranger enter the room and pounced from his chair. He tapped the unsuspecting Baskin on the shoulder and, in his patented fiery tone, ordered him out of the room.

Newman tried to intervene, but the embarrassed Baskin hurried away, leaving Newman and Howell in a heated argument.

A few minutes later, Howell walked over to me in a nearby corner. He was very upset over Newman's verbal attack and then began to question me. "Hey, I might need your advice since you're my new man here, and I might have just screwed up with a House member," Howell began.

"I saw what happened," I told Howell. "What seemed to be the problem?"

"Well, that man went back there, and he's a lobbyist and not a member?" Howell answered.

"Senator Howell, that is Carey Baskin, and he's new out here," I explained. "He's a very nice guy and about as low-key as they come, and he went back there because Bobby Newman motioned for him. He didn't know he was messing up."

"Well, I apologized to Bobby," the senator went on. "I'll find the new man and see if I can explain."

Howell promptly left the room, and I assumed he found Baskin and apologized, but I wouldn't swear to this.

I was able to do a lot of good things in my job, and I was so very thankful for that. It's funny what you remember, and it isn't necessarily the big events. I suppose that's true about life in general, not just a job or two we have along the way. I remember spending the night at the capitol, sleeping in my sleeping bag, watching the snow pile up outside in the parking lot. I had to be at the capitol during legislative sessions because we didn't stop because of inclement weather. So knowing that highways might be closed, I packed my sleeping bag and a toothbrush and slept on the floor in my office in order to be ready for the next day's business.

I also remember driving all night to Biloxi, Mississippi. I was competing in the Arkansas State University golf tournament at Hot Springs, and my Sunday round wasn't completed until 6:30 p.m. Representative Shane Broadway was completing his term as House speaker, and he wanted me to be in Biloxi the following morning to present the Arkansas legislature's official invitation for the Southern Legislative Conference to consider having its next big convention in Little Rock. I was happy that Shane, my friend, wanted me to make the official presentation at the breakfast meeting, so I got in my car after completing my golf round and made the eight-hour drive to Biloxi, where I arrived at 3:00 a.m. I got a little sleep and arrived for the 7:00 a.m. breakfast in plenty of time for my speech. I think they liked what I said because the group's executive committee voted unanimously to accept Arkansas's invitation to be the next host state. After the vote, I went back to my room in the big casino hotel and took a long nap before heading to the slot machines.

The quiet Saturday morning at the capitol, a week before the start of a legislative session—it was hard, getting ready for a session, and the staff worked long hours in advance of the circus coming to town. I was all alone on the south end of the third floor, and I left my office to walk across the marble hallway to the bathroom. On the way, I ran into a man and his young son who were standing outside the big Senate door, peering inside. I greeted them and found out they were from Memphis, that the young boy was in town for a soccer tournament. The man explained that his son had always had an interest in politics and had heard about Bill Clinton. I stopped my work and took them on a private tour, allowing the father to take a photo of his son sitting in the lieutenant governor's chair, the big one in front of the Senate chamber.

We dealt with hundreds of tourists each year at the Senate, and I took time to speak to a lot of the groups, welcoming them into the chamber and taking time to explain the legislative process. But it was a lone tourist I remember the most, a woman from Illinois who stopped me one day on the huge marble staircase outside my office.

"Do you work here?" she asked as we passed each other on the stairs.

"Yes I do," I answered, inquiring further about her visit.

"Oh, what a pleasure it must be, just to work every day in this beautiful, fabulous building," she said.

And I agreed, smiling as I left on my way down the beautiful, fabulous staircase.

Indeed, the Arkansas Capitol Building is a beautiful building, and a lot of people work hard to keep it looking attractive. It is especially attractive at Christmastime when the holiday festivities kick in. Children sing each day at lunchtime, and I tried to steal a little time in the big rotunda to listen to their angelic voices. Christmas carols seem to take on special meaning when children sing them. I listened one day as a young school group from Batesville performed. They were very talented, and I took the time to find out where they were from and the name of the choir director. That afternoon, I dropped a note to the editor of the *Batesville Guard* newspaper just to tell him how much I enjoyed my time listening to the kids' music. The editor liked my note so much he ran it in the paper.

After it appeared, I got a phone call from my buddy, Senator Steve Bell of Batesville. "Scoop, your letter about our school choir ran in the paper up here today," he told me. "I guess you know you just got me reelected for life." We laughed, and I told him I didn't know the letter would go public. He said he was glad it did, and after I thought about it, I was glad too. Maybe the kids needed to know how much I enjoyed their visit and their hard work.

Another feel-good moment of helping people came after I picked up the morning paper and read about US senator David Pryor holding a public hearing in Little Rock. Pryor was near the end of his Washington political career, and he scheduled a public hearing in Little Rock as a part of his effort to draw attention to the rising costs of medical care.

The paper had reported that an elderly couple testified before the panel. The woman said health-care costs had stripped her family of their life savings and that she was even unable to buy ice cream for her ailing husband, the only food he could still eat in his deteriorating condition. The story was heart-wrenching, and after I read it, I picked up the phone and made a call, asking Senator Beebe to drop by my office when he arrived that afternoon.

He came in and asked why I had called. I showed him the newspaper article, and he looked at me, knowing something was on my mind.

"What do you want me to do, Scoop?" he asked in a concerned tone.

"You're close to the Yarnell ice cream folks in Searcy, right?" I asked.

"You bet," he said.

"I want a meeting with them—either you or me—so that we can do something to help this woman."

The following day, a member of the Yarnell family arrived at my office. We arranged for $500 in ice cream coupons to be mailed to the woman, compliments of the ice cream company and Mike Beebe. It was $500, but I went home feeling like a million dollars.

CHAPTER 30

T here were so many memorable events, including Clinton's exit for the presidency, but I'll devote space here to two that always come to mind when I look back on my time inside the Arkansas legislature.

The first was the flip-flopping resignation of Governor Jim Guy Tucker. This occurred in 1996 after the fifty-three-year-old Democrat was found guilty on two counts in a fraud case. The energetic former congressman had become governor in 1992, moving up from lieutenant governor after Clinton ascended to the White House.

Jim Guy was one of the most hardworking men I had ever been around, but he seemed to be mired in a growing number of legal problems, which eventually led to his downfall.

Following his conviction, the time came for him to officially step down as governor and turn the reins over to Lieutenant Governor Mike Huckabee. On July 16, 1996, hundreds of legislators, staff, and observers gathered in the House chamber for Huckabee's swearing in, which had been scheduled for 3:00 p.m. But as we sat and waited in the crowded room, word filtered in that Tucker had changed his mind and had decided to rescind his resignation.

Panic ensued, and hundreds of Huckabee supporters started protesting outside the House chamber and in the crowded halls of the capitol. I was standing near the rear entrance of the House chamber when Senator Stanley Russ of Conway, the Senate pro tem, walked up to me and whispered, "Jim Guy's not resigning."

Senator Steve Bell of Batesville, a close ally of Tucker, then walked up and handed me a note. It said, "He's not resigning. I'm going home to Batesville. Call me."

Chaos followed, and several of us ended up hidden away in Huckabee's small lieutenant governor's office on the second floor of the capitol. All sorts of constitutional queries were flying around, and Huckabee sat and talked with Russ and me and others about what we should do. Calls were placed to Jim Guy Tucker's home, and Russ and I talked with him. In the meantime, research was being done about what, if anything, the legislature could do about possible impeachment proceedings.

Bobby Hogue of Jonesboro, the speaker of the House, announced that he was calling a late-afternoon press conference to address the matter. Russ and I received word that Hogue might call for impeachment proceedings to begin immediately, but these were only rumors.

I talked again with Jim Guy on the phone, and I listened as he explained his reasons for not stepping down. One reason, he said, was that he could appeal his conviction and that the appeal might exonerate him. If this happened, his resignation would have been premature, he said.

I spoke up and said I thought the appeal was not the issue. The issue, I said, was the future of the Democratic Party and what his actions were doing to cause irreparable harm.

In two hours, Secretary of State Sharon Priest announced to the press that Tucker had given her his resignation letter. Speaker Hogue and his lieutenants expressed outrage that Tucker had decided to resign in a letter to the secretary of state rather than informing legislative leaders. Russ asked me about this, and I told him why Tucker had done this. "Because that's who the governor resigns to—the secretary of state," I said.

Huckabee took the reins, and Jim Guy quietly disappeared from the Arkansas political scene, no longer the shining star that had been shining so brightly for so long. Once considered the perfect replacement for Congressman Wilbur Mills, then the US Senate hopeful, then the logical replacement for Governor Clinton . . . gone, in a cloud of chaos and confusion, the Baptist preacher from Texarkana ready and most willing to step into his new place in history.

After the dust settled, I received a very nice letter thanking me for helping everyone through that very long day. It was signed by the new man in charge, Governor Mike Huckabee.

The other memorable day for discussion here is 9-11-2001. Of course, everyone will remember where they were and what they were doing that day. I was driving into work that morning when I heard the initial news bulletins out of New York.

By the time I reached my office, the TV pictures were streaming in, and people were in an understandable panic. The capitol police met with me immediately and explained that bulletins were going out to all public buildings, including state capitols, about possible terrorist attacks.

I assembled my staff and instructed all of them to go home, immediately, and not to return to the capitol building until so instructed. I told them prayers might be a good idea too, since no one seemed to know what our country was facing.

In less than an hour, I was in a meeting with Secretary of State Charlie Daniels, his capitol police, the state police, and Tim Massanelli of the House staff. It was a security briefing on what we would do in case of an attack. The authorities were on high alert, and suspected targets in Arkansas included nuclear plants, air bases, and state and federal buildings. All state capitol buildings around the country were on top alert, we were told.

Besides the aerial attacks, we were briefed on mail packages and what plans were being made in case our offices started receiving dangerous substances through the mail. Every contingency was being discussed because no one really knew the extent of the attacks. Our country had never gone through anything like this, and we were all on edge in trying to cover all the bases.

I was instructed to shut down the Senate and leave the building. The state police or some other authorized authority would be in touch with me when the coast was clear, I was told.

I left the capitol and started my drive home. As I reached the interstate near the Little Rock airport, I looked up and saw more than a dozen large airplanes circling overhead. All planes in America's airspace had been ordered to find the nearest airport immediately, and it was a sight I knew I would never forget. Like everyone else, I felt an urgency and fear unlike anything I had ever experienced. My cell phone rang, and it was Senator Jim Hill, the Senate pro tem, calling from his home in Nashville. I briefed him on what had transpired at the capitol, what the authorities were doing, and what I had been ordered to do. I told him I was driving home and that dozens of big planes were circling above me.

"This is scary, Scoop," he told me.

It sure was scary, and it was something none of us will ever forget.

CHAPTER 31

B efore I wind things up, I thought about offering up my own best and worst list, like the newspapers and magazines used to do. I never did like those articles because I thought some of the selections were unfair, so I thought since I was doing the picking, I would just list my favorites, the legislators I enjoyed working with the most, and leave off the ones I deemed the worst. The list won't include favorite employees like the late Kern Treat, the venerable lawyer who headed the Legislative Council, or favorite constitutional officeholders like Jimmie Lou Fisher, a woman who blazed a lot of trails for women seeking political office. My list is made up of Senate and House members—men and women who became my friends for a number of reasons, but mostly because I liked hanging out with them. And I liked doing that because I believed in them and I trusted them.

The pundits would take me to task if I listed lobbyists among my favorite people, but some of them surely were helpful in my work, and a few are close friends. Those include Tom Kennedy, Don Tilton, Eddie Drilling, Paul "Spook" Berry, Ted Mullenix, Cecil Alexander, Bill Brady, Bill Phillips, Charles Singleton, and the late John Greer. It's true, some lobbyists wined and dined me over the years, but we shared moments and experiences way, way beyond work. They never asked me for an improper political favor, and I know there was a reason for that—they knew better, and they were too professional to do so. So that said, here are my favorite legislators from my time inside the Arkansas legislature.

Mike Beebe of Searcy. No surprise here, people will say, because he did pick me to be the Senate's first chief of staff, a move that changed my life. We became like brothers, and the group of "worms" he surrounded himself with helped rewrite legislative history. He became a great governor too, the first candidate to carry all seventy-five counties. He whacked the awful, regressive grocery tax, and he used his off-the-chart intellect to stabilize a very unstable legislature that set up shop in the early term-limited era of legislative politics. If I had a criticism, it would be some of his appointments to the Game and Fish Commission and that screwy decision by an inept agency that approved a nasty hog farm that threatens our most prized natural resource, the Buffalo River. Preston Bynum, my old Republican friend, called Beebe the best governor in Arkansas history, and Bynum has seen his fair share of 'em. Mike Beebe would have been a wonderful candidate for president, and I say that only because he proved his worth in both the legislative and executive arenas. And he truly was born in a shanty home, on a remote river levee, grew up on the big city streets with only his mother to guide him, and he pulled himself up, dusted himself off, and became an outstanding lawyer and politician. His life story would have been the perfect Hollywood script.

Steve Bell of Batesville. We nicknamed him *Seve* because of his sweet, syrupy golf swing that reminded us of a famous professional golfer. He was shrewd, and he had a laid-back attitude that caught a lot of people off guard. He passed a lot of legislation, like the wily old pro Ode Maddox used to do in the House. He eschewed publicity and the limelight, and he quietly went about his work—becoming one of Beebe's chief lieutenants, a trusted adviser to governors, and my closest legislative friend long after our glory days at the capitol passed—and we had more time for serious pursuits like golf outings and deer hunting. He took a lot of good-natured kidding from the "Worm" group for his early night sleepiness. When some of us were out on the town and just getting started, *Seve* was ready for nighty-night, and that too showed how smart he really was because he felt a lot better than some of us the next morning.

Morril Harriman of Van Buren, Beebe's closest ally and friend. A brilliant lawyer who left Nick Wilson's coterie to hook up with Beebe and the providential decision helped rewrite history at the Arkansas

Senate. If Beebe overlooked something in a bill or in an opponent's clever move, Harriman promptly sniffed it out. It was dizzying to watch the two of them, along with Bell, when they locked on to an issue. Their lawmaking was at supersonic speed. He had a clarity of vision unlike anyone I had ever worked with, and it paid huge dividends for the citizens of Arkansas.

John E. Miller of Melbourne. He opened the door to my legislative career, and I will always owe him for that. Miller was one of the most decisive people I had ever seen. He had a full measure of courage for a little man, and he knew there were people in Arkansas who were down and out, and he kept them in mind when he did his legislating. He agonized over the state's wretched poverty, and he was a religious man but not nutty and overbearing about it like some of his Republican cohorts. His faith didn't prevent him from sharing an off-color joke or two, and those occasional quiet moments over lunch in the speaker's office were some of my very best times. It would have been a good thing if John Miller could have been the full-time speaker of the House because he was a workaholic who tried to move Arkansas forward. He died in 2014.

Wayne Hampton of Stuttgart. I got to know him when I was still working for the *Arkansas Gazette*. My work then led me to his sprawling farm in Arkansas County, where he drove me around as we talked about environmental issues. I was a reporter, and he was a salty old-guard politician—a member of the House at the time but best known for his politics during the Orval Faubus reign. Wayne had headed up the Highway Commission and the Game and Fish Commission, and he had become one of the most influential politicians in Arkansas. We developed a friendship through our environmental work in helping save the Cache River from the dam-happy army engineers. He called me one day, at the *Gazette* office, and said attempts were being made by some of his House colleagues to water down the Freedom of Information law. He said he was opposed to this, but he didn't know how to articulate his concerns in a speech since he was a country farmer who didn't cotton much to public speaking. I asked him why he had called, and he asked if I could write a speech for him, which I did. Perhaps it was a bit of a conflict—me, being a reporter, writing a speech for a politician who would probably end up being praised by my own newspaper for giving such a speech, but I proceeded. The next day, Hampton delivered a stem-winder to stunned colleagues in the House of Representatives, quoting Lincoln and Jefferson, his words electrifying supporters of the free press and the freedom of information cause. After this virtuoso performance, he became the media darling, and the bill to dilute the Freedom of Information law went down in flames. The two of us became even closer friends after that, a friendship that lasted until he was laid to rest in the little country cemetery near his farmhouse. I miss sitting with him and Virginia on the reservoir levee, watching the green-headed mallards flying in for a rest.

George Wimberly of Little Rock. He was the gutsy mayor of Little Rock before he was elected to the House. He died in 2012, a short time after turning ninety and closing down his little drugstore in the Hillcrest section of Little Rock. But of all the people I knew inside the Arkansas legislature, George Wimberly was the most generous and charitable. He gave away a fortune at his little drugstore, which became a hangout for the political elite and the local elderly clientele. Everybody dropped in for medicine and medical advice, and for those shut-ins who were unable to go by, he would deliver their meds to them. I watched one Saturday morning as George carefully removed an ingrown toenail from the Supreme Court justice who had gone in complaining. He was probably the only person who ever served in the Arkansas legislature who gave money away instead of taking it.

Clarence Bell of Parkin. He was like a sweet grandfather, this old football coach who was a seasoned voice for education in his long service in the Senate. He quietly went about his work, always showing that you can get a lot done by being nice rather than posturing like some kind of Max Howell bully. I loved seeing him walk into my office because we could talk forever, about sports, politics, deer hunting, and fishing. I spent some time with him in the fishing boat, and he loved catching goggle-eyes, his favorite tasty treat. People adored him and his wife, whom he affectionately called Bell. He loved his East Arkansas roots and was adamant about sports because he said sports offered young black athletes a chance at success when all other avenues shut down. And he helped me in my battles with obstinate bosses. When a young governor Bill Clinton talked with a group of supporters in his office and sought advice about the well-known car tag controversy, Bell listened quietly as various opinions were offered. Then, he spoke, telling the young governor that controversies are like stepping in cow manure. "When you look down and see cow shit on your boot, it's a lot better not to smear it," the old senator opined. "Let it dry for a while, and then it's much easier to remove." The wise young governor got the message: just leave it alone for a while.

Lloyd McCuiston of West Memphis. Thank goodness he succeeded John Miller as speaker because the little warrior from West Memphis was just what the House needed in the early '80s. He had a remarkable wit, but you didn't want to get on his bad side because he had no time for a regressive attitude. He took the House's image beyond what Cecil Alexander, Jim Shaver, and John Miller accomplished, and he did it in an unassuming, humorous way that everyone loved and appreciated.

David Malone of Fayetteville. He was the quiet senator from Fayetteville, the erudite law professor who served briefly in the House and then moved on to the upper chamber, where he quietly and quickly blossomed. He started the computer revolution in the Arkansas legislature, the first man to carry around a PC. He showed us how this new device could and would change the way we did business. The Arkansas Senate moved quickly into the computer age—the very first state legislative body in the country to do so—and the Senate was space age early because of Malone, the House taking years to follow suit and catch up. Malone was one of the quiet leaders in the Beebe Worm Club that cleverly went to work to dethrone Nick Wilson. And surprisingly, the old law head was a huge Razorback fan and a masterful authority on basketball and football. He accompanied me on many of my Razorback basketball outings to Dallas and Atlanta, and he was a total joy to be with when we stood and called Nolan's championship Hogs.

Jon Fitch of Hindsville. I nicknamed him *Dragline* after he came out publicly against efforts to stop dredging projects on our scenic rivers, but I didn't have a closer friend than Jonathan. We arrived at the capitol at the same time, in the fall of 1978—I being the new House employee and he, a freshman legislator. We shared secrets that only brothers can share, and I sat with him through a lot of heartbreak, much of it in his personal life. He was a terrible golfer, but he loved the game more than Arnold Palmer. No doubt his most enjoyable times were sitting with his fellow Beebe "worms," sharing one of his sissy little umbrella drinks and telling tall tales. Some of us were asked to speak at his funeral, and it was the hardest thing I'd ever done. I'd gone through my own generous doses of heartache, catastrophic injuries, joint replacements, and even cancer, but losing Jon Fitch was a pain I never got over. I told Jim Hill that losing Bill Gwatney was tragic beyond belief, but then losing Jon Fitch a short time later was something I might not be able to handle as a grown man. "I feel the same way, Scoop," Hill said back to me, his voice quivering and tapering off.

Jim Hill of Nashville. He was one of those legislators you really needed to get to know to fully appreciate. He was nondescript, to say the least, but clever and cunning. He was onstage at a big National Conference of State Legislatures meeting in San Antonio with a bunch of other so-called "leaders" from around the country, and who ended up stealing the show—the slow-talking, throat-clearing little white-haired cattle farmer from Nashville, Arkansas, who had the huge audience rolling in the aisle with comments like, "I'd be happy to respond to the House speaker from Pennsylvania, but I honestly didn't understand a cotton-pickin' word he just said." He also had the audience in stitches when he described a temper tantrum as a "duck fit." Like Steve Bell, Hill quietly went about his work and produced in spades. The time I spent with him was some of the best moments in my career, and I am so happy I decided to accept his invitation to stay on and watch him lead the Senate after Beebe moved on. The wiry ex-marine did an admirable job at president pro tem in spite of a scheming band of malcontents who were still loyal to a long-departed Nick Wilson. He died in 2014, and his funeral was highlighted by a huge choir and a tenor whose vocal range shook the big church. The modest Hill would have been embarrassed over such folderol.

Bill Gwatney of Jacksonville. The year 2008 was our group's annus horribilis—Bill Gwatney's inexplicable murder stopping all of us in our tracks, making us cry like small children, hanging overhead like a heavy cloud. I told my friend Richard Mays, the prominent black attorney from Little Rock, that Bill's murder changed me in the most profound way. I said this because few of us uppity, spoiled white boys ever experience a friend or loved one being savagely gunned down. This senseless act made me realize so much more about life, about how poverty and hunger and lost hope can lead people to unbelievable despair, how isolated and protected most of us outside the inner-city strife really are. Who would ever think that a close friend or a relative would become target practice to a pistol-toting crazy man who randomly picked his victims? For no reason, this articulate, handsome, aspiring young businessman, the future leader of the Arkansas Democratic Party, is taken down—for no damn reason at all. Richard Mays had blazed many a civil rights trail in his early days and faced danger, and he knew exactly what I was talking about too because random killings, drive-bys, drug deals gone bad are a frequent nightmarish part of what friends and neighbors in his culture see every day. But Bill Gwatney, Gwatzilla, our little buddy and golf partner, never got the chance to follow Mike Beebe, his mentor, into the governor's chair, and that's exactly the career choice we wanted for him, to succeed Beebe. He was smart, he knew business and taxes, and he had the necessary bipartisan support that would have elevated him above most other candidates. I thought he was a shining star and on the threshold of greatness, and his loss left his family and his Worm Club pals reeling, and his funeral was a day we will never forget.

Preston Bynum of Siloam Springs. When you talk about caring and sensitive people, none rates higher than this stalwart Republican. I met him long before I went to work at the legislature. I was a young reporter for the *Pine Bluff Commercial*, and my assignment was to cover a speech by an up-and-coming young Republican who was speaking at the Holiday Inn. I knew when I met him he had what it takes to be a successful politician, and that is precisely what he turned out to be. He's had countless heart surgeries and medical setbacks, but the unending misfortune never broke his spirit and love for the political process. He was a popular House member and went on to be a very effective lobbyist. He has the rare quality of making you feel like the only person in the room, even when the room is overflowing with people. And honestly, you couldn't find a room big enough if you threw a party for all those loyal to the man *Democrat-Gazette* columnist Meredith Oakley accurately labeled the Gentle Giant.

Bud Canada of Hot Springs. He was the Garland County sheriff for years before moving on to the legislature. He wasn't the most dynamic senator who ever graced the chamber, and he was a little shaky when he talked, but he was effective in getting his legislative agenda over. And he tried for years to remove the sales tax from groceries because he knew it placed a hardship on the poor. Finally, Mike Beebe joined with him in the Senate and got the ball rolling, and Governor Beebe followed through on getting a sharp ax after the dreadful tax.

Bud Canada, like Beebe, came up the hard way, growing up on the streets of Hot Springs. He became an All-American running back for the Arkansas Razorbacks and moved on to a successful pro football career. As a college student, he frequently came home to Hot Springs to drive for Bing Crosby, the famous singer who vacationed in the spa city because of the famous racetrack. The singer gave the young student $100 to drive him around, and that was a lot of money in those days and a lot of money to Bud Canada, who was bordering on destitute status. The stories on Bud are legendary, but I have to tell one. He was a single man and still quite the ladies' man even in old age. He was with his lady friend from New York, and they were dining at Coy's in Little Rock. The woman had to catch a plane at 10:00 p.m., so after dinner, the two of them left to head to the airport. Bud knew all the people at Coy's, and when he walked outside, the young parking attendant said, "Hold on, Senator Canada, I'll bring your car around." In a snap, the young man pulled up in the shiny white Cadillac, and Bud and his friend promptly drove away. He saw her to her plane and began a leisurely stroll back outside, ready to get into his car and head home from the airport. But instead, he was greeted by a fleet of Little Rock policemen, yelling and instructing the shocked and shaking senator to "get on the ground." Bud complied and fell spread-eagle to the pavement. The cops rushed up and started searching him, frantic and screaming.

Finally, one of the older policemen, recognizing Canada from earlier days of law enforcement, said, "Sheriff Canada, is that you?" Bud said yes, and the old cop helped the senator to his feet. It turned out the young parking attendant, in his haste to bring around Canada's white Cadillac, had brought around the wrong white

Cadillac for Bud and his lady friend to drive away from the restaurant. Amazingly, Bud hadn't noticed the difference, and the police had tracked the automobile as stolen and surrounded it at the airport. I couldn't believe Bud wouldn't have noticed the difference in the two cars, and I asked him why he didn't realize he was driving another man's car. "Because I was too busy looking at my pretty date," he told me, laughing.

Tom Kennedy of Russellville. I tell people he's the only senator I ever kissed, this senator turned lobbyist from Yell County. Kennedy came to the Senate and quickly became a big hit with the Beebe team. We could see he was smart and articulate, and he had a sterling reputation as a former prosecuting attorney who was headed places. I say that about the kissing because early in his career, we headed to a favorite restaurant in North Little Rock for an evening meal. We had a big group of people, and the meal was very slow in coming. After several cocktails, Kennedy left the table to walk upstairs to the bathroom. I noticed he had been gone for a while when a young waitress rushed up to our table and asked, "Is there a Mr. Lancaster here?" I answered yes, and she said, "You need to come with me." I followed her up the stairs and could see several people standing in a circle around someone. That someone turned out to be our new young senator, and I raced to his side. He was slumped over a table, coming in and out of consciousness, and I started asking him questions about his health, what he was feeling, had this happened before—things like those. He turned a weird purple color, and I thought he was losing his last breath. I did what I thought I should do, and I started administering mouth-to-mouth, sensing that he was on the verge of dying. Moments later, I looked up and saw that an ambulance crew had arrived, and they moved swiftly, putting him on a stretcher. As the young attendant strapped him down, he looked closely at Tom and said, "Hey, aren't you Tom Kennedy from Russellville?" Turns out the paramedic had grown up in Tom's hometown. They rushed him to the hospital, and I left the emergency room to phone Tom's wife, Kristi, whom I had never met. He left the Senate after a brief stint to become Entergy's chief lobbyist, a post he inherited from the old pro Cecil Alexander. Kennedy became a very close friend and golf partner, and he has suffered through a few more of the scary heart episodes, which caused him to lose consciousness. I wonder what the restaurant people did with all that food we ordered that evening, because all of us ended up at the hospital, too shaken up to think about eating.

Bill Walker of Little Rock. If he reads this, he'll probably laugh that infectious patented laugh of his and say I probably put him on my honky list only because I needed a token minority. That's an inside joke with the two of us because I never dreamed I'd end up liking this man so much. He arrived at the Senate from the House, and before our work together ended, we had engaged in some emotional, heart-to-heart talks about race relations and our hopes for the future. I had followed his House career, and from most accounts, this articulate civil rights advocate was considered a fiery, pompous, bomb-throwing orator who was unwaveringly rigid in his beliefs and political agenda. Some of his early speeches in the Senate made his colleagues uneasy, and he seemed to be isolating himself from every one of his colleagues without really assessing the landscape and knowing that the Senate included a lot of liberal, easygoing white men who were open-minded, not only about race relations, but about almost everything that popped up on their radar. After one such troublesome speech, I asked him to come into my office for a chat, and I began by laying all my cards on the table. I told him I knew his family history, was familiar with his struggles in trying to improve race relations, and that I remembered his father's gallant fight for civil rights. I told him that I was an aging bureaucrat from an all-white town but that my politics and the politics of the Senate leadership were very liberal and open-minded. I think he needed time to figure me out, but we became close, and I never pulled any punches with him.

In one private conversation, I accused my black friend of playing the race card, and he became angry. "When's the last time you had black people over to your house for dinner?' he asked me, trying to make some kind of insightful point.

"Hell, I don't have any black people in my whole hometown to even ask over, and besides, my wife's cooking would probably kill 'em, so what's your point?" I shot back.

"Well, that is my point," he said.

"So now, in order to be open and fair, I have to have black people over to eat with me?" I fired again, adding, "Not everything is political. Please don't make everything political."

At this point, he broke into his patented laugh again, pausing long enough to grin and say, "You all right, you know it."

And Bill Walker was all right too, not only with me but with all of Beebe's entourage. He became one of our brothers and received a much-sought-after position when Beebe became governor. When Jon Fitch gave his swan-song speech upon leaving the Senate, when term limits kicked in, Fitch choked up and recognized his new close friend Bill Walker. Fitch talked about growing up in rural North Arkansas, where there were no blacks, and how he had never even seen a black person until his father brought him to Little Rock in the 1960s for a visit. When Fitch died unexpectedly of a massive stroke, we gathered at the remote cemetery on the Fitch family farm in rural Madison County. One of the pallbearers there to say good-bye was Bill Walker, the tall, handsome black man who had grown in stature, as much or perhaps even more than his white brothers who were weeping along with him on the scenic mountainside.

John Riggs of Little Rock. This millionaire businessman had his Senate career cut short by a screwy redistricting plan that shifted voter strengths to his opponent, but the loss failed to dampen John's enthusiasm for helping shape a better educational system for our state. Like Bill Gwatney and Tom Kennedy, John Riggs could have developed into a magnificent state leader and made a spirited run for governor. He teamed with Beebe's group to offer energy, enthusiasm, and savoir faire, and he picked up on complicated budget issues as quickly as had any person we had ever seen. He was courageous in his speeches and in his voting, and he was a take-no-prisoners kind of guy, standing up to critics with a seldom-seen courage that inspired everyone who watched him work. An avid sportsman and environmentalist, Riggs studied and spoke out on issues that reached far beyond the state borders. If the right opportunity comes along, he may resurface in a political race one day. The anemic Democratic Party of Arkansas sure could use his moxie and decisiveness.

Cliff Hoofman of North Little Rock. He was a key strategist in the Beebe camp's ongoing war against Nick Wilson, and besides his hard-earned law degree, he brought common sense and street smarts to the table. He had blue-collar grit from working hard as a young man in a railroad town, and he was a fierce campaigner—for himself, colleagues, and even Bill Clinton. He shunned the spotlight, especially in the war against Wilson, but he helped draft many of the clever rules that shredded Wilson's committee power. If you wanted to run for office in North Little Rock or Central Arkansas, it was always a good idea to seek Hoofman's aid. It was even better if you could get him to host a fund-raiser at his North Little Rock home and have him cook up some of his tasty frog legs or Cajun dishes. After term limits sent him packing, he served admirably on the Highway Commission and in various judicial circles.

Allen Gordon of Morrilton. He spent his Senate career locked in step with his close friend Nick Wilson, but he was an authoritative voice when it came to technology issues and the growing need to create more four-year colleges. An avid reader, he could talk at length on any subject, and his family's storied political legacy made him a well-connected politician statewide. Like Riggs and Hoofman, he loved the outdoors and spent a lot of his leisure in a favorite trout stream and in the elk country of the Midwest. After his Senate career ended, he became an effective lobbyist and a key player for the attorney general, specializing in legislative issues. Over time, he moved closer to Beebe and his group of friends, and they all moved past the old Beebe-Wilson divide to became regular golfing partners.

Lloyd George of Ola. I couldn't believe it when the sage of Yell County died in 2012. He just seemed invincible, this rugged cattle farmer with the quick wit and keen mind. If anybody could cheat death, it would be the veteran House member who made his colleagues look like they were moving in slow motion or mired in quicksand. He was incredible to watch during the House debates, the way he could manipulate the other ninety-nine. His mind moved in gazelle-type leaps, never stopping even for a split second. His intellect was off the charts, defying his country-bumpkin antics that threw off would-be opponents. He was a highly educated man who tried teaching and coaching before he borrowed enough money to buy a propane company in order to make a better living. He was elected to the House and became a power broker, showing governors how to play the tough political games. He was a genius at work on the House floor, confusing colleagues into voting his way. I watched as the debate swirled around a proposal to start a host of new educational programs that George didn't favor. During a question-and-answer period, he rose and lifted one of the heavy bill books from his desk. "Have y'all even taken time to read this bill?" George asked, slowly raising his voice to imply that the bill might have a hidden agenda. "Listen to me, y'all better read this bill before you vote yes because the way I read it, well, friends, it's going to end up costing this state $37 million more than it already has just to implement." Murmurs all around, and suddenly, a groundswell of concern as the House members picked up on what their veteran colleague was suggesting. When the dust settled, the bill was soundly defeated, and George had spun his magical web once again. Later that evening, I asked George where he came up with the $37 million figure because I couldn't find that figure anywhere in the discussion debate. "Oh, I was just bluffin'," he laughed. "The thirty-seven million dollars—that just sounded scary so I ran with it."

Lloyd became a very close friend, and we remained close until his final days. One afternoon, when I was still working in the House, he walked into my fourth-floor office. "Whatcha doin'?" he asked in his snappy voice.

"I'm working," I answered.

"Let's go outside, I need to see you about something," he said.

"It's one fifteen, Lloyd," I said, explaining that the House had just gone into its afternoon session, and my presence was required on the House floor.

"We'll be right back, let's go," he insisted.

So we walked outside, out the west door of the capitol building, where his four-wheel-drive vehicle was parked. He asked me to step inside, and we sat down in the front seat. That was when he explained his mission. "Let's have a drink," he said.

"A drink? It's one fifteen, Lloyd," I said.

"I don't care. I want a drink."

So I asked what my choices were, and he answered, "Whiskey."

I asked if he had anything I might use to water it down a bit, and he reached into the backseat of the vehicle and snapped up a Diet Dr Pepper. So at one fifteen in the afternoon, with work on temporary hold, I sat in Lloyd George's Chevy Blazer, sipping my Diet Dr Pepper and bourbon.

Mike Ross of Prescott. His first term was not impressive, but with help from Beebe's camp, he grew into a progressive senator who had a solid voting record and an uncanny radar for sensing what was on voters' minds. There was never anyone better at raising money. When he ran his first race, he offended a veteran lobbyist by boldly predicting he would win the race, advising the lobbyist to donate generally. The lobbyist said the brash young candidate told him, "You need to donate to my campaign and get on board because this train is leaving the station." The lobbyist was offended, but he went ahead and donated, and Ross proved over time he could be effective, and that train went all the way to Washington, where it chugged along as a successful, conservative congressman.

David Matthews of Lowell. His tenure in the House was brief, but it didn't take us very long to see the incredible promise of this young attorney. For sure, he was the most articulate orator I observed in my long career, a speechwriter's dream, the way he could take the simplest notion and drive it home with great, unbridled emotion. He chose to cut his career short and go back home to his lucrative law practice. His clients no doubt benefitted greatly from the decision, but the state and the entire legislature suffered a great loss by a promising career cut short.

Carolyn Pollan of Fort Smith. A highly educated, articulate Republican leader who was first-class in her work product and her good looks. She looked like a Hollywood fashion model, but she was tiger tough in her work on behalf of education and human services. She served at a time when there was no partisan rancor, and if there had been, she would have worked to stop it because she used her debate talent and NYU education to address problems without putting others down or putting on a big show. She had a great love for history and worked in her hometown of Fort Smith to help preserve the city's colorful past. She worked briefly for Governor Mike Huckabee, but her glory days were in the House, and they ended, sadly, when term limits sent her packing.

Charlie Cole Chaffin of Benton. Like Pollan, a very strong woman who made her mark in the Senate as a leader in the Democratic Party. She was one of Beebe's people, and she brought one of the brightest minds ever to the upper chamber, not to mention more guts than most of the men she constantly outwitted had. Knox Nelson, the ultimate power broker, was quick to recognize her talent, and he started inviting her to his secretive Sunday afternoon planning sessions out of respect for her debate skills and knowledge of educational issues. She could cuss and drink and shoot the bull on par with her male buddies, and she loved to network, knowing that you can catch a lot of flies with honey. She's also the one who compared Max Howell to a playground bully, and her favorite quote was when she said there "ain't enough guts in the General Assembly to feed a quail a chitlin supper."

Joseph K. "Jodie" Mahony. This El Dorado lawyer was a walking authority on the House rules even though this obsession often distracted him from his real work. He was a member of a prominent politically active family that brought a lot to the table when it came to Arkansas and national politics. Mahony was brilliant, and he had endless energy, which fueled his tenacious work ethic. He roamed the halls of the capitol with a cardboard box full of papers, delving into every kind of issue but concentrating mostly on education. He had a great sense of humor, and he never put himself above others, even though he was wealthy and more intelligent than most around him. What I admired about him was that he didn't put on airs, and like the Kennedys, he chose to make a contribution by participating in public service. He could have quail-hunted in Texas every day (his way of relaxing), stayed home and practiced a little law, sat on the porch with a chew of tobacco (another favorite treat), but he chose to pour himself into a legislative career that turned him into a fierce, competitive, progressive force. He served in the House, then the Senate, and then back to the House. Cancer claimed him far too early.

Percy Malone of Arkadelphia. He is a computer nerd, but he was our computer nerd. A brilliant businessman, Malone has made a ton of money in pharmacy and with his computers, not to mention his valuable cattle. Like David Malone, he was one of the first legislators to sell everyone on the value of computers and how they could improve the legislature's work product. He was invaluable to Bill Clinton early on with computerized campaigning, and he proved invaluable to Jim Hill when the Nashville senator served as pro tem and needed help battling puffed-up insurgents who were obstructionists to good government. He was a steady force for health-care legislation, including help for mental health programs, and he was a strong voice for constitutional rights for individuals, especially minorities who often did not have someone looking after their interests.

Joe Yates of Bentonville. You've read some of my stories now about being with this funny, highly educated Republican with the Ozark Mountain dialect. He liked to put on an act of being a hillbilly, but he had a sharp business mind, and he wanted the state to move forward in education and business. He was a friend of big business, but he also knew how taxes and a poor economy hurt the working man. During one debate on a proposed tax that would hurt the poor and middle class, he spoke up and said, "Let's just go ahead and pass the bill and put the tax on the poor people. They're used to it." One-on-one, there wasn't a more pleasant person to spend quiet time with, whether it was on a deep-sea fishing trip or cooped up in a crowded duck blind. He was a ton of fun every time we were out together for dinner and drinks, and—believe me—that was a lot.

Steve Bryles of Blytheville. He learned quickly that Mike Beebe was the go-to guy if you wanted something accomplished in the Senate. He brought honesty, sharp mind, and quick wit to the table, and he quietly became a top-notch, progressive leader in the Senate by teaming with Jim Hill and Percy Malone. His nickname from high school was "Punkinhead", and it followed him to the Senate, where the moniker was our affectionate way of addressing him. After the legislative career, he stayed with Beebe's team in agricultural work, where he used his wonderful expertise from growing up in cotton country. Like Gwatney and Fitch, he died much too early, succumbing to throat cancer in 2012.

Jimmie Don McKissack of Star City. No one loved serving in the legislature more than this effervescent restaurant owner from Star City, the friendly city. He didn't garner many headlines, and history won't remember him as a standout solon, but he quietly became an effective bill passer. McKissack was a standout in the strong Southeast Arkansas delegation that took their marching orders from Knox Nelson, and he peddled a majority of Nelson's programs in the House, where he cajoled members into following along by being a friendly, easygoing man with an infectious smile that won him a ton of friends. He learned a lot of his skills from his close friend, Cecil Alexander of Heber Springs, who served admirably as both a member and speaker. They remained close friends after their service in the legislature and served admirably together on the state Racing Commission.

Ted Mullenix of Hot Springs. When he first arrived in the House, I thought, *Oh my lord, what have we got here?* He was unsure of himself, and his claim to fame was his cornpone hillbilly act at his country music nightclub. But slowly, he became a respected voice in the Republican Party—and there weren't many of those back then—and he was the first legislator to propose a rainy day fund for the state treasury just in case revenues fell below expectations. As time went on, he became a key member of the strong Hot Springs delegation headed by Bud Canada. After his legislative career ended, he became a very effective lobbyist.

Ray Smith of Hot Springs. He passed away a few years after his legislative career came to an end, but my memory of him remains strong. He was the leading advocate for education in the House for many years and did an excellent job as speaker. He was famous for his long lunch breaks, which included a few sparkling refreshments at a nearby burger pub, and he could deliver some fiery, stem-winder speeches once he returned to the House chamber, refreshed and reinvigorated after those long lunches. He could appear pompous, but his speeches were never about himself—they were always about schoolkids and what was best for them. He was extremely intelligent and one of the very best speech makers ever in the entire General Assembly. The day he left the capitol, I walked down to his first-floor office and helped him pack up. We talked for a while, and then, in typical Ray Smith style, he reached into his small refrigerator and asked, "Do you want to share a cold beer before I leave?" I did just that, and it was an honor, to have just a little more time with a good man who gave a lot to our state.

Bill Ramsey of Prairie Grove. He was a talented singer and musician, but he avoided the legislative spotlight by quietly going about his business in the House. He enjoyed a long career and was one of the most successful members of a strong Northwest Arkansas delegation that pushed hard for area businesses and the University of Arkansas flagship campus. He knew business too because he owned a family clothing store in his progressive little hometown. After his House career, he became a successful lobbyist and representative for the Fayetteville-area Chamber of Commerce, which swung a lot of weight around the capitol. No one was better at forming strong working relationships with fellow legislators, and he was close friends with Preston Bynum, Joe Yates, and Lloyd George—all heavyweights.

John Paul Capps. The Searcy lawmaker served in the House and Senate and was one of the most popular House speakers. He was a darling of the news media because he was one of them—a professional broadcaster who owned his own radio station in his hometown. Jodie Mahony accused him one day during a House debate of using his "mellifluous radio voice" to effectively cut off debate when Jodie wanted to talk more. Jodie was one of the few people in attendance who even knew the meaning of the big word. Capps was a force for good government issues, and you never saw him even close to a controversy, his squeaky-clean image constantly intact and his ethics never in question. He was truly a joy to work with, a wonderful, progressive speaker and a poster boy for good government. The TV cameras loved his handsome face, and I was able to get him on several live telecasts from the House floor.

Mike Kinard of Magnolia. This articulate lawyer brought respectability to the Senate from an area that had been underserved and embarrassed by the actions of some predecessors. Bill Moore had served in the post but fell victim to a series of newspaper articles that accused Moore of attempting to triple-dip reimbursement for travel expenses. One article said Moore attempted to turn in bogus boarding passes for legitimate airline expenses. Kern Treat, the able lawyer who headed up the legislature's Legislative Council, refused to pay Moore, and this led to even more embarrassing publicity. Kinard became an immediate respected voice, studious in his work ethic and quick to join Beebe's growing team. He later served in various judicial positions.

Pat Flanagin of Forrest City. Some folks are probably surprised by this nomination, maybe even Pat, because we were never really close during our time together at the capitol, but I always saw him as a quiet, effective lawmaker who had the state's image at the forefront in his service. He was extremely witty and used his humor to dislodge old ideas and disarm old fogy legislators who stood in the way of progress. He helped his area of the state overcome some of its negatives by being a strong force for education and civil rights. He probably should have stayed longer in public service, maybe even looking at a statewide office or congressional seat, but he moved back home to be with his family, and no one could fault him for that.

Bubba Benton of Little Rock. He might have been the "happiest" of all legislators, always laughing, always with a wonderful, engaging smile. He had his Fordyce roots to ground him and ensure common sense when others in the anemic Pulaski County delegation were going off half-cocked and unable to work their way into leadership positions. He knew banking and finance, and when he wasn't legislating, he was fighting for the oft-forgotten kids at the blind-and-deaf school who needed all the help they could get when it came to slicing up the tasty taxpayer pie.

Jay Bradford, the wild and crazy guy from Pine Bluff, reminds me of a dirt devil cyclone spinning up from a dry field in the Grand Prairie. He is always stewing and brewing and moving. He will go down in history as the man who pulled off the most shocking legislative victory. When redistricting placed him in the same re-election race with Knox Nelson, very few people gave Jay a chance. But those people underestimated his boundless energy and drive. He put his own money in the race and out-campaigned the old pro to claim a shocking victory that changed the entire political landscape in Arkansas. And then he turns around and tells people in Max Howell's hometown that they ought to get themselves a new senator too. Talk about bold! The Democratic Party of Arkansas may be limping along now but it's not because Jay Bradford ever took a back seat. He gives a lot of his own money to the party and there isn't a more loyal Democrat in the Natural State.

Mike Wilson of Jacksonville. This steady-as-you-go House member was a rock of dependability. He was articulate, honest, and a leader who enjoyed a long and distinguished career. A lot like Mahony, Wilson was a successful lawyer and a man of means, coming from a prominent banking family, but he chose public service even when he could have stayed home, practiced law, helped his family of bankers, and squirrel-hunted in the fall, a favorite pastime. He was helpful to members who didn't always know the intricacies of the law and the impact of pending legislation, and this made him popular. When I look in my career rearview mirror, I see Mike Wilson a lot, and I think it's because he was so effective, and he did it in such a quiet, gentlemanly manner.

CHAPTER 32

Those are some of my favorites, and I'll probably look back at the list and wonder why in the world I left off an obvious name or two. Like Charlie Moore or Steve Luelf or John Lipton or Neely Cassidy or my very own brother, Representative Jim Lancaster. But I did my best.

Twenty-six-plus years inside the legislature . . . *whew!* I wouldn't take anything for the experience, but I'm not sure I would have the energy to go back and do any of it again. I grew up at our state capitol in a lot of ways, fighting ol' Max and others, and my hide was leather tough when I departed in 2004. I was a whole lot different from when I went there as a wide-eyed fifteen-year-old errand runner for Mr. Witt. For sure, I met some wonderful men and women, some of whom remain close friends even today. I loved some of the work, and I dreaded other parts of it, but there are perils in every calling. On most days, I couldn't wait to get the day started. On my last day at the capitol, I couldn't wait to leave and put it all behind me.

I wrote their speeches and press releases, assembled and supervised a staff of talented professionals to handle legal concerns and constituency demands, helped clean up and renovate the property, ended some questionable finance procedures, looked after their personal needs and demands, traveled the country to tell others about our advancements, and tried to make them look senatorial and professional even when they acted like spoiled brats and buffoons.

I made mistakes, but I never put my personal needs above the House or Senate, the institutions, even when I accepted a new position to leave one for the other. Well, let me retract that. I was selfish and acted out of personal disgust one time. I walked into a meeting of the Senate Judiciary Committee one morning and observed a familiar face. The man at the microphone was my ex-wife's divorce lawyer and a person I thoroughly and absolutely detested. I asked one of my favorite senators, a committee member, what this lawyer was testifying about, and I was told he was speaking on behalf of a proposal he wanted enacted into law.

"Why, do you have a problem with him?" the senator whispered to me.

"Yeah, anything this guy is for, I'm against," I answered.

With that, the senator raised his hand and offered an immediate motion that the man's idea be tabled. The man knew what had happened, and he knew his idea would never see the light of day as long as I stood watch in the Senate. It might have been wrong for me to do what I did that day, but it sure was a satisfying feeling as I watched the downtrodden lawyer walk toward the exit. He looked back just long enough to see me smile and nod my head, my way of letting him know that I had learned the old Bobby Kennedy lesson of getting even rather than getting mad.

No one doubts that the legislature has changed a great deal—term limits the chief reason—and I got a brief taste of this before I retired and moved back home. Of course, time will tell how an "inexperienced" legislature deals with the mounting problems that come with an ever-expanding government, a powerful executive branch, and the rich special interests that wield incredible influence. But we have to be careful in saying that the new system that limits time served is not as good as the old one because the old one had its share of flaws too, putting far too much power in the hands of ruthless veterans who were swollen with conceit, resistant to change, and quick to order people around like personal slaves.

Maybe a combination of the two would have been the ideal mix, and I honestly think we were about to see just that after Knox Nelson and Max Howell departed and Beebe-led forces moved into power. But the passage of the term limits amendment led to Mike Beebe's departure from the Senate. He loved being a senator, and he probably never would have taken his shot at being governor if he had been able to spend his entire political career in the legislature. His move up may have been bad for the Senate, but it was providential for the governor's office, which got a good man who became extremely popular in his two terms as chief executive.

I do know I got a glimpse at how ineffective an entire 135-member term-limited legislature can be, and it wasn't a pretty sight. Max and Knox and some of the power brokers were long gone, but on some days, the new Senate looked like a *Stooge* movie, a Bud Abbott-Lou Costello who's on first routine. In his first day in the Senate, one rotund booze-hound senator from Hot Springs actually raced to the back of the room to operate his remote-controlled whoopee cushion while impertinent colleagues looked on and roared with laughter. Another new senator rose to sing a "Happy birthday" song to his wife. I stood in amazement, and I could only imagine what Max Howell or Lloyd McCuiston would have done if such reprehensible behavior had occurred on their watch.

It got so bad at one point that a veteran bill writer, who had worked for the Legislative Council for forty years, picked up his briefcase, closed his office door, and walked away from the capitol. He told his secretary he had seen enough, that he would not be back, and that no one need bother planning a going-away party. The man's departure was a huge loss for the legislature—but understandable. He had worked with some of the best, but he couldn't bear to suffer through another single day under the new animal house regime of the early stages of term limits.

We can all be thankful that Mike Beebe, a veteran legislator who knew the ins and outs of the state budget, was the newly elected governor in charge of shepherding along that first class of rancorous, petulant neophytes—the immature kiddie corps—because Beebe had the necessary patience and knowledge to see them off to school, pack them a little lunch, and wipe their snotty noses while they stumbled into their taxpayer-financed playground.

I'll never forget talking with one term-limited House member early in his abbreviated career. He was wide-eyed with excitement, telling me, "You won't believe this, but I've been down there [in Little Rock] nearly a year, and I have yet to pay for a single one of my lunches." I couldn't help but laugh at his naïveté, thinking back to

Knox Nelson days, knowing that Knox not only would have gotten the free lunches—he would have instructed the lobbyist to buy the entire restaurant for him and then picked up a free Lincoln Continental automobile on the way back to the capitol.

Skip Holland, longtime lobbyist for Bell Telephone Company, told the story of how Knox asked the lobbyists to set up a luncheon in Little Rock to plan a fund raiser for the state Literacy Council. Hundreds of people arrived, and the program began when Knox took the microphone and promptly announced he wanted to raise a tidy sum. "And," the veteran senator began in his whispery, Southern drawl, "I see Skip Holland out here in the audience, and, Skip, why don't you stand up and start this thing off by donating the first $10,000." Holland rose to polite applause, waved to the crowd, and smiled at the senator holding the microphone. He also said he promptly wrote out his check for $10,000 and didn't blink an eye.

A second Skip story about Knox put an exclamation point on how controlling the senator could be. Nelson decided the state needed a new trespass law, so he sponsored the bill, which said property owners could post their land by simply painting their property lines with a special purple paint. The bill sailed through and became law, and as things turned out, Knox Nelson's oil company business in Pine Bluff became Arkansas's principal dealer for the new brand of paint. Skip didn't say how much paint his company ended up buying, but he said that when he retired from the phone company, his business had several warehouses full of purple paint if I ever needed some of it. Skip, like the other big-time lobbyists, knew how the game was played.

The first term-limited class was hopelessly lost and lacking in leadership. An important issue was pending in the Senate, and the morning newspaper reported that one key senator was still undecided about his vote. To illustrate his level of indecisiveness, I'll use his quote here in answer to the reporter on how he might vote: "If you're asking me where I stand, I *guess* you could say I'm *fifty-fifty if* I have to vote." How is that for decisive leadership?

My favorite Governor Beebe moment occurred when one inexperienced senator was attempting to drum up support for a harebrained funding proposal. The senator wanted a multimillion-dollar tunnel dug between the capitol and an adjoining building. He said the underground passage would allow legislators and staff to walk between the two buildings and stay out of the rain. Beebe's response to this cuckoo budget-wrecker was this: "Tell the senator to buy an umbrella."

My old friend Don Younts, a retired state capitol policeman, dropped in to see me as I was packing up to leave the Senate in 2004. He told me, "When you get away from here and look back, you'll see what the public sees—they think everybody in politics is a crook." I didn't share my friend's cynicism at the time, but after a while, I did start to feel more cynical. In my twenty-six years at the capitol, I had become so immersed in the system, so indoctrinated, so caught up in myself and my goal to brand and spin our mission that I had lost touch with the real world somewhat. I wasn't as blind to the truth as some of my political bosses who wore boat-paddle-sized blinders, but after moving into a new job away from politics, I began to see politics in a rearview mirror and the Arkansas legislature in a less glamorous light. My old cop friend was right; the general public didn't think very highly of politicians, and who could blame them if they thought the system is rigged and politicians only listened when their hand was out and their palms were greased with lobbyist money?

The future—and whether our state has much of one or, rather, a bright one—will depend on our ability to select the right person to be governor and whether term-limited legislators can use their time wisely now that a new law gives them a little longer time to serve than previously dictated. There will be an occasional legislator who will sparkle, like Bennie Petrus of Stuttgart did in his limited time in the House, but legislators' time will be limited, and they may have fewer and fewer opportunities to spread their wings and fly. As one lobbyist sadly told me, "The term-limited legislators don't know what they don't know."

Some of the first term-limited senators I dealt with from 1999 to 2004 were impulsive, conniving ex-House members who were limited in ability and intellect. They moved in when Senator Beebe's reformers started moving out, and the shoes they stepped into were simply too big to fill. Thankfully, these dimwits are gone, and even less experienced recruits have arrived, but amazingly, the newer ones show much more promise. Republican numbers are soaring, and a growing group of young leaders from this party, including Jonathan Dismang and Jeremy Hutchinson, are taking on more responsibility. Time will tell whether the GOP can move past emotionally charged phobias, such as abortion and guns, and set prejudices aside and, as a *Democrat-Gazette* editorial advised, "show a willingness to see the other fellow's point of view," which many say is the essence of leadership.

All would agree that our state needs responsible leaders, and these new legislators may be able to serve sufficient time under a new term-extending amendment passed in 2014 to adjust to a new system that eschews the massive greed and plundering from the past. We can only hope they remember that character is what flows from the heart and that Arkansas is a unique state and a poor state. They should also remember that not every issue is political, even though we tend to make things this way now.

People involved in politics must be careful not to condemn the new term-limited era outright because the old system, romanticized by some for its tradition and cast of colorful characters, had in some ways become fossilized and stained by corruption—too much power vested in too few and years of questionable meddling and money-grubbing behavior that went unchecked until Beebe-led reformers and the FBI moved in.

So in time, who knows? If some of these term-limited legislators can read up on the constitution and actually do what it says, they may, indeed, earn a greater measure of respect. My hope is that the new legislators will vote their conscience and not be bound by some rigorous, iron-clad pledge put forth by tax-hating special-interest groups who use their mystery money to buy influence. Men and women elected to office are sent to do a job, study the issues, and use their own best judgment in leading, not cowering to rabble-rousing anarchists back home or in a far-away state who always want things their way and only their way.

President Obama hit the nail on the head when he said politicians will never take risks unless the people push them to take risks. David Brooks of the *New York Times* said it best: "Government is not bad—it is good and can be better." And like Faulkner, who looked to the future with shining hope, I see great potential for Arkansas and its legislature, which has as its best friend a budgeting process that keeps our books balanced and our government out of debt.

I never thought I'd quote Max Howell in talking about hope and a better future—or quote him on anything—but in discussing the perplexities of issues, the old man did tell me one thing worth passing along: "Issues are not always black and white," he said. "When a legislator finally has to vote, he needs to remember there are also wonderful shades of gray."

I wrote earlier about my love for Andy Griffith and the lessons we learned from his old TV show. I thought I'd close with an Andy story because I couldn't think of a better way to wind things down.

I was sitting in my office one afternoon when I overheard my secretary talking. She said, "Wait here, and I'll see if he can see you." She walked in and said to me, "A Mr. Thornton is here to see you."

My immediate thought was that my old friend Ray Thornton had dropped in. "Yeah," I said, "ask him to come on back." To my great surprise, in walked Billy Bob Thornton, the Arkansas native turned actor and director. We shook hands, and he explained that he was in town to shoot a movie and that he wanted to film a part of it at our Senate. Of course, I said yes, and we spent the next hour talking about Arkansas, our time growing up in Sheridan and Malvern, and his career in Hollywood. As he turned to leave, he noticed a book on my desk, entitled *Life Lessons from Mayberry*.

"You like Andy Griffith, I see," he said, picking up the book.

"Yes, I sure do," I said.

"How would you like to meet him?" he asked.

"Well, sure, but how would we do that?"

He then explained that one of the star actors in his new film would be Andy Griffith and that filming would begin the following day a few feet outside my office, with Ben Affleck and Andy.

"I'll call you in the morning at nine, and we'll talk," Thornton said as he exited.

The following day, I sat for an hour on the couch with Andy Griffith. We talked about a lot of things—his movie career, the old TV show, the Mayberry characters, and his singing career. "You really do know a lot about me," he said to me in a soft voice that was so familiar.

"Yes, I do," I answered. We parted, and I shook hands with his wife, who leaned over and said, "He loves talking with people who are sincere about his work. He likes you, I can tell."

That experience meant a great deal to me. I remembered what Bill Gwatney had said, that I was "the Andy Griffith of the Arkansas Senate." I was wishing Gwatzilla could have been there in the room with the real Andy and me—and then, I thought, maybe, in some weird, mysterious way I don't understand, he was . . . with us in the room. Or hell, who knows—it might not have been my friend's spirit at all that I was sensing at that moment—it could have been that old Bruce Bennett ghost that Nick Wilson and I had laughed about.

—The End—

"Young Golfers"
Bill Lancaster, Steve Bell and Mike Beebe

Mike Beebe and Bill Gwatney

Jon Fitch and Tom Kennedy

Max Howell, Clarence Bell, Knox Nelson, Ben Allen,
Bill Moore, Paul Benham, Nick Wilson and Bud Canada.
All served as Pro Tem and all but Wilson are deceased

Hotel sign in Hot Springs welcomes "Representative Ron Finch"

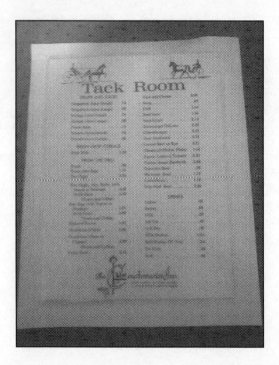

The menu from old Coachman's Inn Tack Room
Restaurant where I dined in 1961

"Scoop" Lancaster, "Skip" Rutherford, "Slick"
Alexander, "Spike" Schaffer and "Spook" Berry

Percy Malone and Don Tilton

President-elect Clinton and Bill Lancaster

Speaker Capps, Speaker McCuiston, Speaker Lipton, Bill
Lancaster, Speaker Buddy Turner and Speaker Ray Smith

Governor Frank White and Bill Lancaster relax at the duck lodge

Bill Lancaster and Congressman Tommy Robinson
at the Max Howell Roast and Toast

Bill Lancaster, Speaker McCuiston, Tim Massanelli and
Jimmie Don McKissack on a fishing trip in 1985

President-elect Clinton says goodbye at the Arkansas Senate to Bill
Lancaster, Clarence Bell, Jim Scott, Wayne Dowd and Joe Yates

Buddy Turner, John Lipton, Lloyd McCuiston, Bill Lancaster
and Mr. and Mrs. Charlie Moore at party in New Orleans

Bill Lancaster in meeting with the "real" Andy
Griffith, star of TV and motion pictures

Bill Lancaster with Governor Mike Beebe

Printed in the United States
By Bookmasters